The
Impossible
is
Possible

JOHN MASON is the founder and president of Insight International, the author of ten books including *An Enemy Called Average*, a minister, and an inspirational speaker. John, his wife, and their four children live in Tulsa, Oklahoma.

You may contact him with your prayer requests or other inquiries at:

John Mason
Insight International
P.O. Box 54996
Tulsa, OK 74155

www.freshword.com
johnmason@freshword.com

JOHN MASON

The Impossible is Possible

BETHANYHOUSE

MINNEAPOLIS, MINNESOTA

The Impossible Is Possible
Copyright © 2003
John Mason

Cover design by Dan Thornberg

Published by Bethany House Publishers
11400 Hampshire Avenue South
Bloomington, Minnesota 55438
www.bethanyhouse.com

Bethany House Publishers is a Division of
Baker Book House Company, Grand Rapids, Michigan.

Printed in the United States of America

Library of Congress Cataloging-in-Publication Data

Mason, John, 1955-
    The impossible is possible : doing what others say can't be done / by John Mason.
      p.   cm.
    ISBN 0-7642-2740-8 (alk. paper)
    1. Christian life.   I.   Title.
    BV4501.3.M277   2003
    248.4—dc21   2003002594

I want to dedicate this book
to my Lord and Savior, Jesus Christ.
In the potter's hand, He makes
something out of nothing.
Thank you, Father, for your
faithfulness, grace, and mercy.
To God be the glory.

To my awesome wife, Linda,
and my great kids,
Michelle, Greg, Mike, and Dave,
thanks for all your support,
love, and laughter.

TABLE OF CONTENTS

INTRODUCTION

ALMOST EVERYTHING WE ENJOY TODAY was impossible yesterday. So what transforms an impossibility into a possibility, a possibility into a probability, and a probability into a fact?

Deep inside you lives an impossible thought. A dream longing to come true. There's a mission residing in you, put there by your heavenly Father. You see, He specializes in the impossible. That's where He is at His best. He is able to do more than we can ask or think.

Life can be a perpetual barrage of "things" coming at us, beside us, and past us. Fear, faith, friends, envy, the past, greed, giving, serving, mistakes, anger, peace, indecision, and love ask for our time and demand our attention. What they can leave is an impression that everything is impossible, or at least very difficult.

The good news is that God wants to do more than we can imagine. He longs to take our impossibilities and turn them into possibilities. In this book I want to introduce you to God's view of our life. When a mistake makes a situation impossible, God can turn it around. When worry wants to paralyze us, God wants to bring us freedom. When confusion seems to be the only answer, God wants to shed light on His path for us.

Perhaps there is no greater truth than that "with men this is impossible, but with God all things are possible" (Matthew 19:26 NASB).

Safety Last!

FOR MANY YEARS, "'Safety first' has been the motto of the human race . . . but it has never been the motto of leaders. A leader must face danger. He must take the risk and the blame and the brunt of the storm" (Herbert Casson). If you want to be successful, you must either have a chance or take one. You can't get your head above water if you never stick your neck out.

A dream that does not include risk is not truly worthy of being called a dream. Lord Halifax said,

> *The man who leaves nothing to chance will do few things [badly], but he will do very few things.*

If you never take risks, you'll never accomplish great things. Everybody dies, but not everyone has lived.

C. S. Lewis said,

> *The safest road to hell is a gradual one— the gentle slope, soft under foot, without sudden turnings, without milestones, without sign posts.*

Elizabeth Kenny reflected, "It is better to be a lion for a day than a sheep all your life." If you dare for nothing, you need hope for nothing.

If you don't risk anything, you risk even more. John Newman wrote, "Calculation never made a hero." Every person has a chance to improve himself, but some just don't believe in taking chances. I agree with Lois Platford, who said, "You have all eternity to be cautious and then you're dead." Being destined for greatness requires that you take risks and confront great hazards.

You'll always miss 100 percent of the shots that you don't take. I agree with John Stemmons:

> *When your chances are slim and none . . .*
>   *go with slim.*

Morris West said, "If you spend your whole life inside waiting for the storms, you'll never enjoy the sunshine." No one reaches the top without daring.

Listen to Conrad Hilton:

> *I encourage boldness because the danger of*
> *seniority and pension plans tempt a young man to*
> *settle in a rut named security rather than*
> *find his own rainbow.*

Chuck Yeager remarked, "You don't concentrate on risk. You concentrate on results. No risk is too great to prevent the necessary job from getting done."

Whenever you see a successful person, I guarantee he or she took risks and made courageous decisions. Success favors the bold. The world is a book where those who do not take risks read only one page. David Mahoney said, "Refuse to join the cautious crowd that plays not to lose. Play to win."

Pietro Metastaisio observed,

> *Every noble acquisition is attended with its risk;*
> *he who fears to encounter the one must not*
> *expect to obtain the other.*

Listen to Tommy Barnett: "Many people believe that you are really walking by faith when there is no risk, but the truth is the longer you walk with God ... the greater the risk." If you have found yourself throughout life never scared, embarrassed, disappointed, or hurt, it means you have never taken any chances.

David Viscot wrote, "If your life is ever going to get better, you'll have to take risks. There is simply no way you can grow without taking chances." You have a chance to improve yourself. Just believe in taking chances.

IF GOD IS YOUR FATHER, PLEASE CALL HOME

PRAYER BRINGS MOMENTUM. It lifts the heart above the challenges of life and gives it a view of God's resources of victory and hope. Prayer provides power, poise, peace, and purpose for a person's purpose, plans, and pursuits. The most powerful energy anyone can generate is prayer energy.

The devil smiles when we make plans.
He laughs when we get too busy.
But he trembles when we pray.
—CORRIE TEN BOOM

Don't worry about anything; instead,
pray about everything; tell God your needs
and don't forget to thank Him for his answers.
If you do this, you will experience God's peace,
which is far more wonderful than
the human mind can understand.
—PHILIPPIANS 4:6–7 TLB

Whatever is worth worrying about is certainly worth praying about. God is never more than a prayer away from you. When you feel swept off your feet, get back to your knees.

*If I could hear Christ praying for me
in the next room, I would not fear a million
enemies. Yet distance makes no difference.
He is praying for me.*

—ROBERT MURRAY MCCHEYNE

Heaven is ready to receive you when you pray. "Time spent in communion with God is never lost" (Gordon Lindsay).

*I have so much to do today that I shall
spend the first three hours in prayer.*

—MARTIN LUTHER

Common people do not pray, they only beg. So pray, don't beg. When we pray, we link ourselves with God's inexhaustible power and insight. "Wishing will never be a substitute for prayer" (Edwin Louis Cole).

Remember that prayers can't be answered until they are prayed. "Whatever things you ask when you pray, believe that you receive them, and you will have them" (Mark 11:24 NKJV).

A day hemmed in prayer is less likely to unravel.

—ANONYMOUS

When we pray, we must simultaneously position ourselves to be willing to take the action that God requires as answers to our prayer because "prayer is not monologue but dialogue; God's voice in response to mine is its most essential part" (Andrew Murray). The prayers a person lives on his feet are no less important than those he says on his knees.

*Practical prayer is harder on the soles of your shoes
than on the knees of your trousers.*

—OSTEN O'MALLEY

The strongest action that you can take in any situation is to go to your knees and ask God for help. The highest purpose of faith or prayer is not to change my circumstances but to change me. Pray to do the will of God in every situation—nothing else is worth praying for.

> *Do not have your concert and*
> *tune your instruments afterwards.*
> *Begin the day with God.*
>
> —JAMES HUDSON TAYLOR

Prayer may not change all things for you, but it sure changes you for all things. Prayer is the stop that keeps you going. If God is your Father, please call home.

Fear Wants You to Run From Something That Isn't After You

THE GREAT EVANGELIST BILLY SUNDAY once said,

Fear knocked at my door. Faith answered . . .
and there was no one there.

Now, that's the proper response to fear. Fears, like babies, grow larger by nursing them. Benjamin Disraeli offered, "Nothing in life is more remarkable than the unnecessary anxiety which we endure, and generally create ourselves." We must act in spite of fear . . . not because of it. If you are afraid to step up to the plate, you will never hit a home run.

Lucy Montgomery said, "It only seems as if you are doing something when you are worrying." Worry doesn't help tomorrow's troubles, but it does ruin today's happiness.

A day of worry is more exhausting
than a day of work.

—JOHN LUBBOCK

When you worry about the future, there will soon be no future for you to worry about. No matter how much a person dreads the future, he usually wants to be around to see it. Unfortunately, more people worry about the future than prepare for it.

Never trouble trouble until trouble troubles you. Arthur Roche said,

> *Worry is a thin stream of fear trickling through the mind. If encouraged, it cuts a channel into which all other thoughts are drained.*

Sister Mary Tricky observed, "Fear is faith that it won't work out." Instead, do what the book of 1 Peter admonishes:

> *Let him (God) have all your worries and cares, for he is always thinking about you and watching everything that concerns you.*

Rob Gilbert advised, "It's all right to have butterflies in your stomach. Just get them to fly in formation."

Fear holds you back from flexing your risk muscle, so consider this: What you fear about tomorrow is not here yet. George Porter warned, "Always be on guard against your imagination. How many lions it creates in our paths, and so easily! And we suffer so much if we do not turn a deaf ear to its tales and suggestions."

Worry is like a darkroom, because darkrooms are where negatives are developed. If you can't help worrying, remember worrying can't help you either. Worry is like a rocking chair: It keeps you going but you don't get anywhere. A friend of mine said, "Don't tell me that worry doesn't do any good. I know better. The things I worry about don't happen."

Worry never fixes anything. Shakespeare wrote, "Our doubts are traitors, and they make us lose what we oft might win, by fearing to attempt."

Emanuel Celler says, "Don't roll up your pant legs before you get to the stream."

Most of our fears can be traced back to a fear of man. However, the Bible says that "fear of man brings a snare" (Proverbs 29:25 NKJV).

The Lord is the strength of my life;
of whom shall I be afraid?

—PSALM 27:1

In God I trust; I will not be afraid.
What can mortal man do to me?

—PSALM 56:4 NIV

People would worry less about what others think of them if they only realized how seldom they do. They're not thinking about you—they're wondering what you're thinking about them.

Fear can keep you from going where you could have won. Don't let your fears steal from you and prevent you from pursuing your dream. Most people believe their doubts and doubt their beliefs. So do like the old saying: "Feed your faith and watch your doubts starve to death." Worry is a route that leads from somewhere to nowhere; never let it direct your life. Fear of the future is a waste of the present. Fear not tomorrow . . . God is already there!

Never be afraid to trust an unknown future
to a known God.

—CORRIE TEN BOOM

A famous poem says it best:

Said the robin to the sparrow,
I should really like to know
Why these anxious human beings
Rush about and worry so.

Said the sparrow to the robin,
I think that it must be
That they have no Heavenly Father
Such as cares for you and me.

GET UP ONE MORE TIME THAN YOU'VE FALLEN DOWN

HAVE YOU EVER FAILED or made a mistake? Good, then this nugget is for you. The fact that you've failed is proof that you're not finished. Failures and mistakes can be a bridge, not a barricade, to success.

Psalm 37:23–24 says,

The steps of a good man are ordered by the Lord: and he delighteth in his way. Though he fall, he shall not be utterly cast down: for the Lord upholdeth him with his hand.

Failure may look like a fact, but it's only an opinion. Successful people believe that mistakes are just feedback. It's not how far you fall but how high you bounce that makes all the difference.

Theodore Roosevelt said,

Far better it is to dare mighty things, to win glorious triumphs, even though checkered by failure, than to rank with those poor spirits who neither enjoy much nor suffer much because they live in the great twilight that knows not victory or defeat.

One of the riskiest things you can do in life is to take too many precautions and never have any failures or mistakes. Failure is the opportunity to start over more intelligently.

No one has ever achieved genuine success who did not, at one time or another, teeter on the edge of disaster. If you have tried to do something and failed, you are vastly better off than if you had tried to do nothing and succeeded. The person who never makes a mistake must get awfully tired of doing nothing. If you're not making mistakes, you're not risking enough.

Vernon Sanders observes,

> *Experience is a hard teacher because she*
> *gives the test first, the lesson afterwards.*

Experience is what you get when you are looking for something else.

Success consists of getting up just one time more than you fall down. So get up and go on.

"You don't drown by falling in the water, you drown by staying there," said author Ed Cole.

Proverbs 28:13 (TLB) reminds,

> *A man who refuses to admit his mistakes can never*
> *be successful. But if he confesses and forsakes them,*
> *he gets another chance.*

The death of your dream will not happen because of a failure; its death will come from indifference and apathy. The best way to go on after a failure is to learn the lesson and forget the details. If you don't, you'll become like the scalded dog that fears hot water and, afterward, fears cold as well.

Failure can become a weight, or it can give you wings. The only way to make a comeback is to go on. If the truth were known, 99 percent of success is built on former failure. A mistake usually proves somebody stopped talking long enough to do something.

You're like a tea bag: not worth much until you've been through some hot water.

Remember the old poem:

> *Success is failure turned inside out,*
> *The silver tint of the clouds of doubt.*
> *And you never can tell how close you are;*
> *It may be near when it seems so far.*
> *So stick to the fight when you're hardest hit;*
> *It's when things seem worse*
> *that you must not quit.*
>
> —UNKNOWN

Even Postage Stamps Become Useless When They Get Stuck on Themselves

IF YOU ARE ONLY LOOKING OUT FOR YOURSELF, look out! Wesley Huber said, "There is nothing quite so dead as a self-centered man—a man who holds himself up as a self-made success, and measures himself by himself and is pleased with the result." Is your favorite letter "I"? Listen:

The core of sin is "I" no matter how you spell it.
—ED COLE

The only reason pride lifts you up is to let you down.

Some time ago when I answered the phone, the voice on the other end said, "Bang! You're dead!" I paused. I didn't know what to think about what had been said to me. Then I heard the familiar voice of James Campbell, a client of mine, saying, "John, just calling to remind you that we need to die to ourselves every day."

This is true. There is always room at the top for anyone who is willing to say, "I'll serve," and means it. Several years ago I was listening to Zig Ziglar, whose presentation included the words

You'll always have everything in life
that you want if you'll help enough
other people get what they want.

When I heard this, something went off inside me. I made a conscious decision to incorporate that concept into my life. It has made a tremendous difference.

True leadership always begins with servanthood, while selfishness always ends in self-destruction. John Ruskin said,

When a man is wrapped up in himself,
he makes a pretty small package.

Being a servant is not always the most natural thing to do. We are all conditioned to think about ourselves. That is one reason 97 percent of all people will write their own names when they are offered a new pen to try. Despite our tendency toward self-promotion, it is always true that more is accomplished when nobody cares who gets the credit.

God has always called us to serve those whom we lead. Be willing to serve without trying to reap the benefits. Before looking for a way to get, look for a way to give. No one is truly a success in life until he or she has learned how to serve. The old saying is true:

The way to the throne room is
through the servants' quarters.

One of the most powerful decisions you can make in your life is to do something for someone who does not have the power or resources to return the favor. In Matthew 23:11, our Lord says, "He that is greatest among you shall be your servant." And, in Matthew 20:26–27, He declares,

Whosoever will be great among you, let him
be your minister; and whosoever will be
chief among you, let him be your servant.

When you give of yourself to help other people, you cannot help but be abundantly rewarded. Norman Vincent Peale observed, "The man who lives for himself is a failure. Even if he gains much wealth, power or position he is still a failure." Conceit makes us fools:

> *Do you see a man wise in his own eyes?*
> *There is more hope for a fool than for him.*
> —PROVERBS 26:12 NIV

The man who believes in nothing but himself lives in a very small world. The best way to be happy is to forget yourself and focus on other people. Henry Courtney said,

> *The bigger a man's head gets,*
> *the easier it is to fill his shoes.*

A swelled head always proves there is plenty of room for improvement.

"The greatest magnifying glasses in the world are a man's own eyes when they look upon his own person" (Alexander Pope). Egotism is the only disease where the patient feels well while making everyone else around him feel sick. Egotism blossoms but bears no fruit. Those who sing their own praises seldom receive an encore. Charles Elliot intones,

> *Don't think too much of yourself. Try to cultivate*
> *the habit of thinking of others; this will reward you.*
> *Selfishness always brings its own revenge.*

While gazing upon selfish accomplishments, the arrogant often miss God by failing to see what He is doing. Rick Renner said, "Don't miss the plan of God by self-consumption."

When you are on a high horse, the best thing to do is to

dismount at once. You can't push yourself forward by patting yourself on the back. Burton Hillis remarked, "It's fine to believe in ourselves, but we mustn't be too easily convinced." An egotist is his own best friend. The fellow who is deeply in love with himself should get a divorce.

Another famous poem describes it well:

> *When days are hot and flies are thick,*
> *Use horse sense—cooperate.*
> *This is a truth all horses know;*
> *They learned it many centuries ago.*
> *One tail on duty at the rear*
> *Can't reach that fly behind the ear.*
> *But two tails when arranged with proper craft*
> *Can do the job, both fore and aft.*

People who boast of being self-made usually have a few parts missing. You can recognize a self-made man; his head is oversized, and he has arms long enough to pat himself on the back. A conceited person never gets anywhere because he thinks he is already there. Change your favorite word from "I" to "You."

CLIMB OUT OF THE GRANDSTAND AND ONTO THE PLAYING FIELD

YOU CAN'T FULFILL YOUR DESTINY on a theory ... it takes *work*! None of the secrets of success will work unless you do. You are made for action. Success simply takes good ideas and puts them to work. What the *free enterprise* system really means is that the more enterprising you are, the freer you are. What we all need is less emphasis on *free* and more on *enterprise*.

Listen to Shakespeare: "Nothing can come of nothing." A belief is worthless unless converted into action. The Bible, a book of faith, talks about work over five hundred times. Often, the simple answer to your problems is: *Go to work.*

> *Striving for success without hard work is like trying to harvest where you haven't planted.*
> —DAVID BLY

What you believe doesn't amount to very much unless it causes you to wake up from your dream and start working. You cannot just dream yourself into what you could be. The only time a lazy person ever succeeds is when he tries to do nothing. An old saying says it best: "Laziness travels so slowly, poverty soon overtakes it."

When you are lazy, you must work twice. It is always a trying time for the person who is always trying to get something for nothing. Did you notice? We weren't given apple juice, we were given apples. Some say *nothing* is impossible, yet there are a lot of people doing *nothing* every day.

Some do things while others sit around becoming experts on how things might be done. The world is divided into people who do things and people who talk about doing things. Belong to the first group—there is far less competition.

"All men are alike in their promises. It is only in their deeds that they differ" (Moliére). Wishing has never made a poor man wealthy. Robert Half nails it:

> *Laziness is the secret ingredient that goes into failure, but it's only kept a secret from the person who fails.*

The faith to move mountains always carries a pick. Rising above mediocrity never just happens; it is always a result of faith combined with works.

Faith without works is like gold within the earth: It is of no value until it is mined out. A person who has faith but no actions is like a bird that has wings but no feet. James 2:17 says, "Even so faith, if it hath not works, is dead, being alone."

Biblical principles multiplied by nothing equal nothing.

We need to be people who put our faith into action. One individual with faith and action constitutes a majority. Do not wait for your ship to come in; swim to it! Thomas Edison said it best:

> *Opportunity is missed by most people because it is dressed in overalls and looks like work.*

True faith has hands and feet; it takes action. It is not enough to *know that you know*. It is more important to *show that you know*.

More precisely, words for "work" appear 564 times in the Bible; therefore, work is a scriptural concept. When faith and work operate together, the result is a masterpiece. We should choose to keep our faith working all the time. George Bernard Shaw mused,

When I was young, I observed that nine
out of every ten things I did were failures.
So I did ten times more work.

Kemmons Wilson, the founder of Holiday Inn, replied to those who asked him how he became successful by saying, "I really don't know why I'm here. I never got a degree, and I've only worked half days my entire life. I guess my advice is to do the same, work half days every day. And it doesn't matter which half. The first twelve hours or the second twelve hours."

Tap into the power that is produced when faith is mixed with action, and then watch God move in your situation.

Tell yourself:

Inspirations never go in for long engagements;
they demand immediate marriage to action.
—Brendan Francis

If the truth were known, most of our troubles arise from loafing when we should be working, and talking when we should be listening.

There is a man in the world
    Who never gets turned down,
Wherever he chances to stray;
    He gets the glad hand in the populous town,
Or out where the farmers make hay;
    He is greeted with pleasure on deserts of sand,
And deep in the isles of the woods;
    Wherever he goes there is a welcoming hand—
He's the man who delivers the goods.
—Walt Whitman

Your Best Friends Are Those Who Bring Out the Best in You

TELL ME WHO YOUR BEST FRIENDS ARE, and I will tell you who you are. If you run with wolves, you will learn how to howl, but if you associate with eagles, you will learn how to soar to great heights. Proverbs 27:19 (TLB) says, "A mirror reflects a man's face, but what he is really like is shown by the kind of friends he chooses." The simple but true fact of life is that you become like those with whom you closely associate—for the good and the bad. Think about it; almost all of our sorrows spring out of relationships with the wrong people. Instead,

Keep out of the suction caused by
those who drift backwards.

—E. K. PIPER

The less you associate with some people, the more your life will improve. Any time you indulge mediocrity in others it increases your mediocrity. A Bulgarian proverb confirms, "If you find yourself taking two steps forward and one step backwards, invariably it's because you have mixed associations in your life." If a loafer isn't a nuisance to you, it's a sign that you are somewhat of a loafer yourself. I have discovered that an important attribute in successful people is their impatience with people who think and act negatively. Misery wants your company. But you don't have to let it in the door. Proverbs 13:20 tells us,

> *He that walketh with wise men shall be wise;*
> *but a companion of fools shall be destroyed.*

We become like those with whom we associate.

We need to be careful of the kind of insulation we use in our lives. We do need to insulate ourselves from negative people and ideas, but we should never insulate ourselves from godly counsel and wisdom.

A number of years ago I found myself at a stagnation point in my life; I was unproductive and unable to see God's direction clearly. One day I noticed that almost all of my friends were in the same situation. When we got together, our problems were what we talked about. As I prayed about this matter, God showed me that I needed "foundation-level" people in my life. Such individuals bring out the best in us and influence us to improve. They cause us to have greater faith and confidence and to see things from God's perspective. After being with them, our spirits and our sights are raised.

The Lord showed me that I needed to change my closest associations and that I needed to have contact with the right people on a regular basis. These were men of strong faith, people who made me a better person when I was around them. They were the ones who saw the gifts in me and could correct me in a constructive, loving way. My choice to change my closest associations was a turning point in my life.

I have found that it is better to be alone than in the wrong company. A single conversation with the right person can be more valuable than years of study.

When you surround yourself with the right kind of people, you enter into the God-ordained power of agreement. Ecclesiastes 4:9–10, 12 (TLB) states,

> *Two can accomplish more than twice as much as one, for the results can be much better. If one falls, the other pulls him up; but if a man falls when he is alone, he's in trouble. . . . And one standing alone can be attacked and defeated, but two can stand back-to-back and conquer; three is even better, for a triple-braided cord is not easily broken.*

Steer clear of negative-thinking experts. Remember: In the eyes of average people, average is always considered outstanding. Look carefully at your closest associations, because it's an indication of the direction you're heading.

There's Nothing in the Middle of the Road but Yellow Stripes and Dead Armadillos

—James Hightower

"MY DECISION IS MAYBE—and that's final." Is this you? Being decisive is essential for a successful life. If you deny yourself commitment, what will you do with your life? Every accomplishment, great or small, starts with a decision.

Choice, not chance, determines destiny. You can't get a hit with the bat on your shoulder. Nothing great was ever done without an act of decision. Too many people go through life not knowing what they want but feeling sure they don't have it. Herbert Prochnow said, "There is a time when we must firmly choose the course which we will follow, or the relentless drift of events will make the decision for us."

People often are like wheelbarrows, trailers, or canoes: They need to be pushed, pulled, or paddled. You're either moving other people to decisions or they're moving you. Decide to do something now to make *your* life better. The choice is yours.

David Ambrose remarked,

If you have the will to win, you have achieved half your success; if you don't, you have achieved half your failure.

Lou Holtz said,

If you don't make a total commitment to whatever you are doing then you start looking to bail out the first time the boat starts leaking. It's tough enough getting the boat to shore with everybody rowing, let alone when a guy stands up and starts putting his life jacket on.

The moment you definitely commit yourself, God moves as well. All sorts of things happen to help you that never would have otherwise occurred. Edgar Roberts said, "Every human mind is a great slumbering power until awakened by a keen desire and a definite resolution to do." Kenneth Blanchard observed,

There is a difference between interests and commitment. When you are interested in doing something, you only do it when it is convenient. When you are committed to something, you accept no excuses, only results.

Lack of decisiveness has caused more failures than lack of intelligence or ability.

Maurice Witzer said, "You seldom get what you go after unless you know in advance what you want." Indecision often gives an advantage to the other person because he did his thinking beforehand. Helen Keller said,

Science may have found a cure for most evil; but
it has found no remedy for the worst of them all—
the apathy of human beings.

Joshua encouraged, "Choose for yourselves this day whom you will serve" (Joshua 24:15 NIV). Don't leave a decision for tomorrow that needs to be made today.

Bertrand Russell said, "Nothing is so exhausting as indecision, and nothing is so futile." Likewise, Joseph Newton discerned,

Not what we have, but what we use,
not what we see, but what we choose—
these are things that mar or bless human happiness.

Remember, don't be a middle-of-the-roader, because the middle of the road is the worst place to try to go forward. As James Hightower quipped, "There's nothing in the middle of the road but yellow stripes and dead armadillos." You can do everything you ought to do—once you make a decision. Today, decide on your dream.

There Is No Future in the Past

IF YOU LOOK BACK TOO MUCH, you'll soon be heading that way. Mike Murdock said, "Stop looking at where you have been and start looking at where you can be." Your destiny and call in life is always forward, never backward. Katherine Mansfield advised,

> *Make it a rule of life never to regret and*
> *never to look back. Regret is an appalling waste*
> *of energy. You can't build on it. It's only good*
> *for wallowing in.*

Consider the words of the apostle Paul:

> *Forgetting those things which are behind*
> *and reaching forward to those things which are*
> *ahead . . . I press toward the goal for the prize*
> *of the upward call of God in Christ Jesus.*
> —Philippians 3:13–14 NKJV

You are more likely to make mistakes when you act only on past experiences. Rosy thoughts about the future can't exist when your mind is full of the blues about the past.

A farmer once said his mule was awfully backward about going forward—this is also true of many people today. Are you backward about going forward? Phillip Raskin said, "The man who wastes today lamenting yesterday will waste tomorrow lamenting today." Squash the "good old days" bug.

The past is always going to be the way it was. Stop trying to change it. Your future contains more happiness than any past you can remember. Believe that the best is yet to come.

> *Though no one can go back and make*
> *a brand new start, anyone can start from now*
> *and make a brand new ending.*
> —CARL BARD

Consider Oscar Wilde:

> *No man is rich enough to buy back his past.*

Take note of what W. R. Ing said: "Events in the past may be roughly divided into those which probably never happened and those which do not matter." The more you look back, the less you will get ahead. Thomas Jefferson was right when he said, "I like the dreams of the future better than the history of the past." Many a has-been lives on the reputation of his reputation.

Hubert Humphrey mused,

> *The good old days were never that good, believe me.*
> *The good new days are today, and better days*
> *are coming tomorrow. Our greatest songs*
> *are still unsung.*

When you are depressed, you will find that it is because you are living in the past. What's a sure sign of stagnation in your life? When you dwell on the past at the expense of the future, you stop growing and start dying. Note Ecclesiastes 7:10 (NKJV):

> *Do not say, "Why were the former days*
> *better than these?" For you do not*
> *inquire wisely concerning this.*

I agree with Laura Palmer's advice: "Don't waste today regretting yesterday instead of making a memory for tomorrow." David McNally reminded, "Your past cannot be changed, but you can change your tomorrow by your actions today." Never let yesterday use up too much of today. It's true what Satchel Paige said: "Don't look back. Something may be gaining on you."

"Living in the past is a dull and lonely business; looking back strains the neck muscles, causing you to bump into people not going your way" (Edna Ferber). The first rule for happiness is to *avoid lengthy thinking on the past.* Nothing is as far away as one hour ago. Charles Kettering added,

> *You can't have a better tomorrow if you are*
> *thinking about yesterday all the time.*

Your past doesn't equal your future.

Procrastination Is the Fertilizer That Makes Difficulties Grow

ASK YOURSELF: "IF I DON'T TAKE ACTION NOW, what will it ultimately cost me?" When a procrastinator has finally made up his mind, the opportunity has usually passed by. Edwin Markum said,

> *When duty comes a knocking at your gate,*
> *   Welcome him in; for if you bid him wait,*
> *He will depart only to come once more*
> *   And bring seven other duties to your door.*

What you put off until tomorrow, you'll probably put off tomorrow too. Success comes to the man who does today what others were thinking of doing tomorrow. The lazier a man is, the more he is going to do the next day.

> *All problems become smaller if you don't*
> *dodge them, but confront them. Touch a thistle*
> *timidly, and it pricks you; grasp it boldly,*
> *and its spines crumble.*
>
> —William Halsey

Wasting time wastes your life. Miguel de Cervantes pondered, "By the street of By and By, one arrives at the house of never." A lazy person doesn't go through life—he's pushed through it. "The wise man does at once what the fool does finally" (Balthasar Gracian).

"Someday" is not a day of the week. Doing nothing is the most tiresome job in the world. When you won't start, your difficulties won't stop. Tackle any difficulty now—the longer you wait the bigger it grows. Procrastinators never have small problems because they always wait until their problems grow up.

In the game of life nothing is less important than the score at halftime.

> *The tragedy of life is not that man loses,*
> *but that he almost wins.*
>
> —HAYWOOD BROUN

Don't leave before the miracle happens! Robert Louis Stevenson commented that "saints are sinners who kept on going." The race is not always to the swift but to those who keep on running. Some people wait so long the future is gone before they get there.

The first step to overcoming procrastination is to eliminate all excuses for not taking action. The second step is not to be so busy! Everyone is always on the move. People are moving forward, backward, and sometimes nowhere at all, as though they were on a treadmill. The mistake most people make is in thinking that the main goal of life is to stay busy. This is a trap. What is important is not whether you are busy but whether you are progressing; the question is one of activity versus accomplishment.

A gentleman named John Henry Fabre conducted an experiment with processionary caterpillars, so named because they have a habit of blindly following each other no matter how they are lined up or where they are going. In his research, Fabre placed these tiny creatures in a circle. For twenty-four hours the caterpillars dutifully followed one another around and around and around. Then Fabre placed the caterpillars around a saucer full of

pine needles (their favorite food). For six days the mindless creatures moved around and around the saucer, dying from starvation
and exhaustion even though an abundance of choice food was
located less than two inches away. The caterpillars were extremely
active, but they were not accomplishing anything.

We should be known as those who accomplish great things for
God—not as those who simply talk about it. Procrastinators are
good at talking, not doing. Mark Twain said,

> *Noise produces nothing. Often a hen who has
> merely laid an egg cackles as though she
> has laid an asteroid.*

We must be like the apostles. These men are not known for their
policies, procedures, theories, or excuses but for their acts. Many
people say that they are waiting for God, but in most cases God is
waiting for them. Together with the psalmist, we need to say, Lord,
"my times are in your hands" (Psalm 31:15 NIV).

The cost of growth is always less than the cost of stagnation.
As Edmund Burke warned,

> *The only thing necessary for the triumph of evil
> is for good men to do nothing.*

Occasionally you may see someone who doesn't do anything
though appearing to be successful in life. Don't be deceived.
Remember the old saying: "Even a broken clock is right twice a
day."

Most people who sit around waiting for their ship to come in
often find it is hardship. Those things that come to a man who
waits seldom turn out to be the things he's waited for. The hardest
work in the world is that which should have been done yesterday.
Hard work is usually an accumulation of easy things that should
have been done last week.

Sir Josiah Stamp said, "It is easy to dodge our responsibilities, but we cannot dodge the consequences of dodging our responsibilities." William James reflected, "Nothing is so fatiguing as the eternal hanging on of an uncompleted task." When people delay action until all factors are perfect, they do nothing. Jimmy Lyons mused, "Tomorrow is the only day in the year that appeals to a lazy man."

Procrastination is the grave in which opportunity is buried. Anybody who brags about what he's going to do tomorrow probably did the same thing yesterday. Few things are more dangerous to a person's character than having nothing to do and plenty of time in which to do it. Killing time is not murder, it's suicide. Two things rob people of their peace of mind: Work unfinished, and work not yet begun.

The Bible promises no loaves to the loafer.

> *A man with nothing to do does far more strenuous "labor" than any other form of work. But my greatest pity is for the man who dodges a job he knows he should do. He is a shirker, and boy! What punishment he takes . . . from himself.*
> —E. R. COLLCORD

Carve out a future; don't just whittle away the time.

Stay Out of
Your Own Way

HERE'S THE FIRST RULE OF WINNING: Don't beat yourself. Your biggest enemy is you. Have you felt like Dwight L. Moody when he said, "I have never met a man who has given me as much trouble as myself"? The first and best victory is to conquer you.

Very often a change of self is needed more than a change of scenery. Here's some good advice: Only you can hold yourself back; only you can stand in your own way. There is no one to stop you but you.

Talk back to your internal critic. "If you want to move your greatest obstacle, realize that your obstacle is yourself—and that the time to act is now" (Nido Cubein).

You must begin to think of yourself as becoming the person you want to be:

> *Give the man you'd like to be*
> *a look at the man you are.*
> —EDGAR GUEST

Change what you tell yourself, for "no one really knows enough to be a pessimist" (Norman Cousins).

Remember, "One of the nice things about problems is that a

good many of them do not exist except in our imaginations"
(Steve Allen). The fear you fear is only in yourself and nowhere
else.

Most of the important battles we face will be waged internally.
There are two forces warring against each other inside us. One
says, "You can't!" while the other says, "With God, you can!" Be
encouraged by this fact found in the book of Matthew: "With God
all things are possible."

"It's not the mountain that we conquer, but ourselves" (Sir
Edmund Hillary). The basic problem most people have is that they
are doing nothing to solve their basic problem, which is that they
build a case against themselves—they are their own worst enemy.

What we are, good and bad, is what we have thought and
believed. Therefore, don't put water in your own boat; the storm
will put enough in on its own. Don't dream up thousands of reasons why you can't do what you want to; find one reason why you
can. It is easier to do all the things you should do than spend the
rest of your life wishing you had.

We lie loudest when we lie to ourselves. "You can't consistently
perform in a manner that is inconsistent with the way you see
yourself," says Zig Ziglar. Determine to multiply your commitment, divide your distractions, subtract your excuses, and add your
faith. The first key victory you must win is over yourself: "Stay out
of your own way" (David Blunt).

SMILE—IT ADDS TO YOUR FACE VALUE

THERE IS A FACE-LIFT you can perform yourself that is guaranteed to improve your appearance. It's called a smile. Laughter is like changing a baby's diaper—it solves a problem and makes things more acceptable for a while. Cheer up! A dentist is the only person who is supposed to look down in the mouth. Robert Frost observed,

Happiness makes up in height
for what it lacks in length.

Abraham Lincoln said, "Most folks are about as happy as they make up their minds to be." The worst day that you can have is the day you have not laughed.

The optimist laughs to forget; the pessimist forgets to laugh. You might as well laugh at yourself once in a while—everyone else does. The only medicine that needs no prescription, has no unpleasant taste, and costs no money is laughter.

A smile is a curve that you throw at someone else, and it always results in a hit. A smile goes a long way, but you're the one that must start it on its journey. Your world will look brighter from behind a smile.

Henry Ward Beecher said,

*A person without a sense of humor is like
a wagon without springs—jolted by
every pebble on the road.*

Take to heart the words of Moshe Waldoks:

*A sense of humor can help you overlook the
unattractive, tolerate the unpleasant, cope with the
unexpected, and smile through the unbearable.*

Your day goes the way the corners of your mouth turn. I believe that every time you smile, and even much more so when you laugh, you add something to your life. A smile is a curve that helps us see things straight. Janet Layne said,

*Of all the things you wear, your
expression is the most important.*

Proverbs 17:22 says, "A merry heart doeth good like a medicine." A good laugh is the best medicine, whether you are sick or not.

"The world is like a mirror; frown at it, and it frowns at you. Smile and it smiles too" (Herbert Samuel). Every man who expects to receive happiness is obligated to give happiness. Cheerfulness is contagious, but it seems like some folks have been vaccinated against the infection. The trouble with being a grouch is that you have to make new friends every month.

Our attitude always tells others what we expect in return. Happiness is an inside job. He who laughs, lasts. Smile often and give your frown a rest.

A smile is a powerful weapon. It can break the ice in tough situations. It will help you keep a proper perspective on life. Helen Keller said,

Keep your face to the sunshine,
and you cannot see the shadow.

You will find that smiling is like having a head cold; both are very catchy. A laugh a day will keep negative people away. As enthusiasm increases, stress and fear decrease. The Bible says that the joy of the Lord is our strength (Nehemiah 8:10).

Cranks do not turn the wheels of progress. Tom Walsh says,

Every minute your mouth is turned down
you lose sixty seconds of happiness.

Paul Bourge wrote, "Unhappiness indicates wrong thinking, just as ill health indicates a bad regime." It's impossible to smile on the outside without feeling better on the inside. If you can laugh at it, you can live with it.

It was only a sunny smile,
But it scattered the night.
Though little it cost in giving,
It made the day worth living.

—ANONYMOUS

There's No Excuse for Being Full of Excuses

"NINETY-NINE PERCENT OF FAILURES come from people who have a habit of making excuses" (George Washington Carver). You are never a failure until you begin to blame somebody else. Stop blaming others. You'll find that when you become good at making excuses you won't be good at anything else. Excuses are the tools a person with no purpose or vision uses to build great monuments of emptiness.

You can learn from your mistakes if you don't waste your time denying and defending them:

> *It seems to me these days that people who admit they're wrong get a lot further than people who prove they're right.*
> —Deryl Pfizer

What poison is to food, alibis are to a productive life. Proverbs says that "work brings profit; talk brings poverty."

> *Some men have thousands of reasons why they cannot do what they want to do when all they really need is one reason why they can.*
> —Willis Whitney

One of the biggest alibis is regret. Don't leave any regrets on the field—give your all in the game of life. "The most valuable thing I have learned from life is to regret nothing" (Somerset Maugham).

Eliminate your regrets, for the truth is that a thousand regrets do not pay one debt.

> *Regret is an appalling waste of energy; you can't build on it. It's only good for wallowing in.*
>
> —KATHERINE MANSFIELD

When a winner makes a mistake, he says, "I was wrong"; when a loser makes a mistake, he says, "It wasn't my fault." Do you admit, "I was wrong," or do you say, "It wasn't my fault?" A winner explains; a loser explains away.

Idle people lack no excuses. The word *can't* usually means you won't try. *Can't* weakens our resolve and many times does more harm than slander or lies. *Can't* is the worst excuse and the foremost enemy of success.

We have many reasons for failure but not a real excuse. "Excuses always replace progress" (Ralph Waldo Emerson). Philippians (2:14–15 TLB) gives wonderful guidance:

> *In everything you do, stay away from complaining and arguing, so that no one can speak a word of blame against you.*

Alibis and excuses should be cremated, not embalmed. The person who excuses himself always accuses himself. Denying a fault doubles it.

The best years of your life are the ones in which you decide your problems are your own. You don't blame them on your mother, the ecology or the president. You realize that you control your own destiny.

—ALBERT ELLIS

Don't buy the alibi. We should live our lives like Florence Nightingale, who said, "I attribute my success to this: I never gave or took an excuse."

ALWAYS SAY LESS
THAN YOU KNOW

RECENTLY I SAW A SIGN under a mounted largemouth bass: "If I had kept my mouth shut I wouldn't be here." How true! Don't jump into trouble mouth-first.

What we say is important. The book of Job reminds us, "How forcible are right words." Let me pose this question for you: What would happen if you changed what you said about your biggest problem, your biggest opportunity?

Our daily commitment ought to be, "Oh, please, fill my mouth with worthwhile stuff, and nudge me when I've said enough." The human tongue is only a few inches from the brain, but when you listen to some people talk, mouth and mind seem miles apart. The tongue runs fastest when the brain is in neutral.

A high school track coach was having difficulty motivating his athletes to perform at their best. The team had developed the distinctive reputation of coming in last at every meet they entered. One factor contributing to the coach's less-than-successful program was his pep-talk tactic. His most effective inspiring tool, he thought, was to tell his team, "Keep turning left and hurry back." Would that motivate you? Remember: Your words have the power to start fires or quench passion.

We should not be like the man who joined a monastery in which the monks were allowed to speak only two words every seven years. After the first seven years had passed, the "new" initiate met with the abbot, who asked him, "Well, what are your two words?"

"Food's bad," replied the man, who then went back to his silence.

Seven years later the clergyman asked, "What are your two words now?"

"Bed's hard," the man responded.

Seven years later—twenty-one years after his initial entry into the monastery—the man met with the abbot for the third and final time. "And what are your two words this time?" the abbot asked.

"I quit."

"Well, I'm not surprised," the cleric answered disgustedly. "All you've done since you got here is complain!"

Don't be known as a person whose only words are negative. Choose to speak positive, motivating, pleasant words. Blaise Pascal commented,

Kind words do not cost much. They never blister the tongue or lips. Mental trouble was never known to arise from such quarters. Though they do not cost much, yet they accomplish much. They bring out a good nature in others. They also produce their own image on a man's soul, and what a beautiful image it is.

Sir Wilfred Grenfell said, "Start some kind word on its travels. There is no telling where the good it may do will stop."

The words "I am . . ." are potent words; be careful what you hitch them to. The thing you're claiming has a way of reaching back and claiming you.
—A. L. KITSELMAN

Sometimes your biggest enemies and most trustworthy friends are the words you say to yourself. As Proverbs says, "Life and death are in the power of the tongue."

Henry Ward Beecher reflected,

A helping word to one in trouble is often like the switch on a railroad track ... an inch between a wreck and smooth rolling prosperity.

Johann Lavater advised, "Never tell evil of a man if you do not know it for certain, and if you know it for certain, then ask yourself, 'Why should I tell it?' "

What words have the most powerful effect on you? George Burnham said, " 'I can't do it' never accomplished anything. 'I will try' has performed wonders."

If your lips would keep from slips;
   Five things observe with care;
      To whom you speak, of whom you speak,
      And how, and when, and where.
                    —ANONYMOUS

Paths Without Obstacles Don't Lead Anywhere Important

TO GET TO THE "PROMISED LAND," you'll have to navigate your way through the wilderness. All of us encounter obstacles, problems, and challenges across our paths, and our decisions as to how we respond to them and view them are significant.

> *Dear brothers, is your life full of difficulties and temptations? Then be happy, for when the way is rough, your patience has a chance to grow. So let it grow, and don't try to squirm out of your problems. For when your patience is finally in full bloom, then you will be ready for anything, strong in character, full and complete.*
>
> —JAMES 1:2–4 TLB

A man with twenty challenges is twice as alive as a man with ten. If you haven't got any challenges, you should get down on your knees and ask, "Lord, don't you trust me anymore?" So what if you've got problems—that's good! Why? Because consistent victories over your problems are important steps on your stairway to success. Be thankful for challenges, for if they were less difficult, someone with less ability would have your job.

"A successful man will never see the day that does not bring a fresh quota of problems, and the mark of success is to deal with them effectively" (Lauris Norstad).

> *You will never be the person you can be if pressure, tension and discipline are taken out of your life.*
> —JAMES BILKEY

Refuse to let yourself become discouraged by temporary setbacks. If you are beginning to encounter some hard bumps, don't worry. At least you are out of a rut. Circumstances are not your master.

You can always measure a man by the amount of opposition it takes to discourage him. When the water starts to rise, you can also. You can go over, not under! "Obstacles across our path can be spiritual flat tires—disruptions in our lives seem to be disastrous at the time, but end by redirecting our lives in a meaningful way" (Bernie Siegel).

The truth is, if you find a path with no obstacles, it is most likely a path that doesn't lead anywhere important. Adversity is the mother of invention, and man's adversity is always God's opportunity. Difficulty gives birth to opportunity:

> *"In this world you will have trouble. But take heart! I have overcome the world."*
> —JOHN 16:33 NIV

"What is the difference between an obstacle and an opportunity? Our attitude towards it. Every opportunity has a difficulty, and every difficulty has an opportunity" (J. Sidlow Baxter). "Show me someone who has done something worthwhile, and I'll show you someone who has overcome adversity" (Lou Holtz). Many people have good intentions, but when something bad comes their way they simply stop. Every path has a puddle, but puddles can be the tools by which God shapes us for better things.

Remember, the travel is worthy of the travail when you're on the right road. If we would just recognize that life is difficult, things would be much easier.

> *Every problem has in it the seeds of*
> *its own solution. If you don't have any*
> *problems, you don't get any seeds.*
> —NORMAN VINCENT PEALE

Watch out for emergencies—they are your big chance! Live your life so that you can say, "I've had a life full of challenges, thank God!"

THE NOSE OF THE BULLDOG IS SLANTED BACKWARD SO HE CAN CONTINUE TO BREATHE WITHOUT LETTING GO

—WINSTON CHURCHILL

PERSISTENT PEOPLE BEGIN THEIR SUCCESS where most others quit. We Christians need to be known as people of persistence and endurance. One person with commitment, persistence, and endurance will accomplish more than a thousand people with interest alone. In Hebrews 12:1 (NIV) we read:

> *Therefore, since we are surrounded by such a great cloud of witnesses, let us throw off everything that hinders and the sin that so easily entangles, and let us run with perseverance the race marked out for us.*

The more diligently we work, the harder it is to quit. Persistence is a habit—so is quitting.

Never worry about how much money, ability, or equipment you are starting with; just begin with a million dollars' worth of determination. Remember: It's not what you have; it's what you do with what you have that makes all the difference. Many people eagerly begin "the good fight of faith" but then forget to add patience, persistence, and endurance to their enthusiasm. Josh Billings said,

> *Consider the postage stamp. Its usefulness consists in its ability to stick to something until it gets there.*

You and I should be known as postage-stamp Christians.
In 1 Corinthians 15:58, the apostle Paul writes,

> *Therefore, my beloved brethren, be ye steadfast, unmovable, always abounding in the work of the Lord . . . your labor is not in vain in the Lord.*

Peter tells us, "Wherefore, beloved, seeing that ye look for such things, be diligent that ye may be found of him in peace, without spot, and blameless" (2 Peter 3:14). And wise Solomon points out, "Do you see a man skilled in his work? He will serve before kings" (Proverbs 22:29 NIV).

> *The nose of the bulldog is slanted backward so he can continue to breathe without letting go.*

In the Far East, people plant a tree called the Chinese bamboo. During the first four years, they water and fertilize the plant with seemingly little or no results. Then, in the fifth year, they again apply water and fertilizer—and in five weeks' time the tree grows ninety feet in height! The obvious question is, "Did the Chinese bamboo tree grow ninety feet in five weeks or five years?" The answer is five years. If at any time during those five years the people had stopped watering and fertilizing the tree, it would have died.

Many times our dreams and plans appear not to be succeeding.

We are tempted to give up and quit trying. Instead, we need to continue to water and fertilize those dreams, nurturing the seeds of the vision God has placed within us. If we do not quit, if we display perseverance and endurance, we will also reap a harvest.

By perseverance the snail reached the ark.

—CHARLES HADDON SPURGEON

An Original Is Hard to Find but Easy to Recognize

HOW MANY OUTSTANDING PEOPLE do you know with unique and distinctive characteristics? They're *different*. I believe that one of the greatest compliments you can receive is for someone to come up to you and say, "You're different!" I'm not suggesting that you be weird for weirdness's sake. Be yourself, and you will stand out.

Don't be a living custard. It's true what Eric Hoffer said:

When people are free to do as they please, they usually imitate each other.

Man is the only creation that refuses to be what he is.

Don't be awestruck by other people and try to copy them. Nobody can be you as efficiently and as effectively as you can. One of the hardest things about climbing the ladder of success is getting through the crowd of copies at the bottom.

The number of people who don't take advantage of their talents is more than made up for by the number who take advantage of the talents they scarcely have. Begin to accept the way God made you.

You are a specialist. You are not created to be all things to all people. More than 90 percent of all flowers have either an unpleasant odor or none at all. Yet it is the ones with a sweet fragrance that we tend to remember. Stand out!

> *Following the path of least resistance is*
> *what makes men and rivers crooked.*
> —LARRY BIELAT

Too many people make cemeteries of their lives by burying their talents and gifts. These abilities are like deposits in our personal accounts, and we get to determine the interest. The more interest and attention we give them, the more valuable they become.

The copy adapts himself to the world, but the original tries to adapt the world to him. It doesn't take a majority to make a change—it takes only a few determined originals and a sound cause. I agree with the old saying that says, "You're the only one in all of creation who has your set of abilities. You're special . . . you're rare. And in all rarity there is great worth."

> *Could Hamlet have been written by a committee,*
> *or the Mona Lisa painted by a club? Could the*
> *New Testament have been composed as a*
> *conference report? Creative ideas do not spring*
> *from groups. They spring from individuals.*
> —A. WHITNEY GRISWOLD

Each of us has our own unique, individual way. There are no precedents; you are the first *you* that ever was. You are the most qualified person on the face of the earth to do what you are destined to do.

WHEN GOD IS ALL YOU HAVE, THEN HE IS ALL YOU NEED

YOU CAN FIND GOD! But there is a condition: Seek Him with all your heart. You will always get into trouble when you try to handle your life without God. Second Chronicles 32:8 (NIV) reads:

> *With us is the Lord our God to help us*
> *and to fight our battles.*

God, the ultimate warrior, lives in you. If you are a soldier for Christ, don't worry about public opinion. Only be concerned about your Commander's opinion. If you fear God, there is no need to fear anything else.

I believe we should follow Mary Lyons' advice: "Trust in God and do something." Satan doesn't care what we worship as long as we don't worship God. Too many people ask the Lord to guide them and then grab the steering wheel. Your relationship with God will last if He is first in your life. Often people want God's blessing, but they don't want Him.

When you lose God, it is not God who is lost. Some people talk about finding God as if He could have lost His way. The Bible says, "Draw near to God and He will draw near to you" (James 4:8 NKJV). William Law added,

*Nothing has separated us from God, but our
own will, or rather our own will is our
separation from God.*

Tommy Barnett reflected, "The deeper I dig, the deeper He digs."
To increase value, get to know God. Pray to the Father, "I want to
be in your will, not in your way."

Oswald Chambers advises us:

*Get into the habit of dealing with God about every-
thing. Unless in the first waking moment of the day
you learn to fling the door wide back and let God
in, you will work on a wrong level all day; but
swing the door wide open and pray to your
Father in secret, and every public thing
will be stamped with the presence of God.*

Stop every day and put Him first.

The Bible finds us where we are, and with our permission it
will take us where we ought to go. Other books were given to us
for information, but God's Word was given to us for transforma-
tion. A person who merely samples the Word of God never
acquires much of a taste for it. Instead, choose to be a wholly
devoted follower of Him. Our heartfelt cry to God ought to be the
same as Isaiah's cry: "Here am I, send me!" (Isaiah 6:8 NIV). Consider the words of W. H. Atken:

*Lord, take my lips and speak through them;
take my mind and think through it; take
my heart and set it on fire.*

We must not only give what we have, we must also give what we
are to God.

ARE YOU READY?

TO ONE PERSON THE WORLD IS desolate, dull, and empty; to another the same world looks rich, interesting, and full of meaning. "Eyes that look are common. Eyes that see are rare," says J. Oswald Sanders. How we position ourselves to receive makes all the difference. You can never see the sunrise by looking to the west. The choice is up to you.

If you look at life the wrong way there is always cause for alarm. It's the same way a twenty-dollar bill can look so big when it goes to church and so small when it goes for groceries. What you see depends mainly on what you look for. Some people complain because roses have thorns. Instead, be thankful that thorns have roses.

Position yourself to receive, not resist. How you see things on the outside of you depends on how things are on the inside of you.

> *Any fact facing us is not as important as our attitude toward it, for that determines our success or failure.*
>
> —NORMAN VINCENT PEALE

Don't pray for rain if you're going to complain about the mud.

"You and I do not see things as they are. We see things as we are" (Herb Cohen). Develop the hunter's approach, the outlook that wherever you go there are ideas waiting to be discovered. When you are positioned right, opportunity presents itself. Opportunities can drop in your lap if you have your lap where opportunities drop.

Opportunity can be missed if you are broadcasting when you should be tuning in. When opportunity knocks, some people object to the interruption.

> *One of the greatest and most comforting truths is that when one door opens, another closes, but often we look so long and regretfully upon the closed door that we do not see the one that is open for us.*
> —Anonymous

See success where others see only failure. Expect something good to happen—that expectation will energize your dreams and give them momentum. You'll gain the advantage by doing things before they need to be done—positioning yourself ahead of time. You'll enjoy ongoing success when you travel in advance of the crowd.

I believe one of the major benefits of reading great books is that they can teach us how to respond beforehand to many of life's challenges and opportunities. Great information can lead you to "dig a well before you are thirsty and plant a seed before you are hungry."

The trouble with the future for most people is that it arrives before they are ready for it. Positioning yourself to receive causes you to be ready. Are you ready?

You'll find that life responds to your outlook. We go where our vision is. Life is mostly a matter of expectation.

THE SECRET TO LIVING
IS GIVING

ONE WAY TO ESTEEM A PERSON is by what he says. A *better* way is by what he does. The *best* way is by what he gives. Elizabeth Bibesco said,

> *Blessed are those who can give without remembering and take without forgetting.*

The big problem is not the haves and have-nots; it's the give-nots. The Lord loves a cheerful giver—and so does everyone else.

Charles Spurgeon urged, "Feel for others—in your wallet." An Indian proverb says, "Good people, like clouds, receive only to give away."

The best generosity is that which is quick. When you give quickly, it is like giving twice. When you give only after being asked, you have waited too long.

Whatever good happens in your life is not so that you can keep it all to yourself. Part of it is intended to be given to others. I agree with E. V. Hill:

> *Whatever God can get through you,*
> *He will get to you.*

The book of Acts says, "It is more blessed to give than to receive" (20:36). Giving is always the thermometer of our love for others. Eleanor Roosevelt observed, "When you cease to make a contribution, you begin to die." Getters don't receive happiness. Givers do.

Living for others is the best way to live for yourself. John Wesley advised, "Make all you can, save all you can, give all you can." That's an excellent formula for a successful life.

When it comes to giving, some people stop at nothing. The trouble with too many people who give until it hurts is that they are so sensitive to pain. Greed always diminishes what has been gained. Mike Murdock states, "Giving is proof that you have conquered greed."

If you have, give. If you lack, give. G. D. Bordmen said, "The law of the harvest is to reap more than you sow." It is true: People who give always receive.

Selfishness continually ends in self-destruction.

Henry Drummond said, "There is no happiness in having or in getting, but only in giving." The test of generosity is not necessarily how much you give but how much you have left. Henry David Thoreau said, "If you give money, spend yourself with it." What you give, lives.

YOUR PROBLEM IS
YOUR PROMOTION

EVERY OBSTACLE INTRODUCES A PERSON to himself. How we respond to obstacles is of ultimate importance.

The greatest example of the right response to an obstacle in the Bible is in the story of the giant Goliath, who confronted and intimidated the armies of Israel, including the brothers of a young shepherd named David. David's brothers chose not to do anything about the obstacle before them, but David did. What was the difference? The way each viewed the problem. The brothers looked at the obstacle and figured it was too big to hit, but David looked at the obstacle and figured it was too big to miss.

The way you look at any obstacle in your life makes all the difference.

Let each new obstacle force you to go to the next level with God. No obstacle will ever leave you the way it found you. You will be better, or you will be worse.

Keep in mind this important fact about obstacles: Every obstacle has a limited life-span. We worried about things last year that we can't even remember today. Don't believe the devil when he tells you that things will not change, that they will not pass.

Obstacles subdue mediocre people, but great leaders rise above them. You and I need to be like the great man who, when asked what helped him overcome the obstacles of life, responded, "the other obstacles." We should be like a kite that rises against the wind. Every problem has a soft spot; there *is* an answer.

Many people think most of their obstacles are money-related, but the correct perspective is to know that a problem that can be solved with a checkbook is not really an obstacle; it's an expense.

Someone said that obstacles are what we see when we take our eyes off the goal. Keep your eyes on the goal and remember that you are not alone in your struggle.

> *We know that in all things God works for the good of those who love him, who have been called according to his purpose.*
> —ROMANS 8:28 NIV

In times of adversity, you don't have an obstacle; you have a choice. In the midst of unbelievable circumstances, believe. God's got a promotion for you.

THE KEY TO MY SUCCESS IS HIDDEN IN MY DAILY ROUTINE, SO TODAY I WILL . . .

KNOW THAT TODAY IS THE DAY that I prayed for.

Make myself valuable to somebody.

Say "thank you" and "please."

Not lose an hour in the morning, then spend all day looking for it.

Tackle a problem bigger than me.

Compliment someone.

Look for miracles coming toward me and by me.

Get to better know God by reading His Word.

Make a small improvement in some area.

Help someone who has no opportunity to repay me.

Change my thinking from TGIF to TGIT—"Thank God It's Today."

Choose to love God and celebrate people.

Do at least three things that will take me out of my comfort zone.

Know that the devil hates this new day because I'm up again.

Die to myself.

Give thanks for my daily bread.

Leave others a little better than I found them.

Observe that every day the earth praises the Lord.

Rise early because no day is long enough for a day's work.

Not be afraid to ask for help.

Give my best time of the day to communion with God.

Live by the Golden Rule so I will never have to apologize for my actions tomorrow.

Do today what I want to put off until tomorrow.

Know that the place to be happy is here—the time to be happy is now.

Take small steps to conquer a bad habit.

Evaluate my actions not by the harvest but by the seeds I plant.

WHEN YOU MAKE YOUR MARK IN LIFE, YOU WILL ALWAYS ATTRACT ERASERS

TO SUCCEED IN LIFE YOU MUST OVERCOME the many efforts of others to pull you down. How you choose to respond to criticism is one of the most important decisions that you make.

The first and great commandment about critics is, *Don't let them scare you.* Charles Dodgson warned,

> *If you limit your actions in life to things that nobody could possibly find fault with, you will not do much.*

Nothing significant has ever been accomplished without controversy, without criticism. When you allow other people's words to stop you, they will.

Christopher Morley said, "The truth is, a critic is like a gong at a railroad crossing, clanging loudly and vainly as the train goes by." Many great ideas have been lost because people who had them couldn't stand the criticism and gave up. A critic is someone who finds fault without a search warrant. Fault is absolutely one of the easiest things to find.

The most insignificant people are those most apt to sneer at others. They are safe from reprisals, and have no hope of rising in their own esteem but by lowering their neighbors.

—WILLIAM HAZLITT

Critics not only expect the worst but also make the worst of what happens.

Dennis Wholey advised,

Expecting the world to treat you fairly because you are a good person is a little like expecting a bull not to attack you because you are a vegetarian.

I agree with Fred Allen when he said, "If criticism had any real power to harm, the skunk would have been extinct by now." Remember this about a critic: A man who is always kicking seldom has a leg to stand on. Great minds discuss ideas, good minds discuss events, and small minds discuss other people.

The Bible says to multiply, but too many critics prefer to divide. Don't allow yourself to become a critic. Jesus warns, "Judge not, that ye be not judged" (Matthew 7:1). You will always make a mountain out of a molehill when you throw dirt at other people. No mud can soil you except the mud you throw. The mud tosser never has clean hands.

You can't carve your way to success with cutting remarks. You will never move up if you are continually running someone down. As Tillotson mused,

There is no readier way for a man to bring his own worth into question than by endeavoring to detract from the worth of other men.

Henry Ford commented,

> *Men and automobiles are much alike. Some are right at home on an uphill pull; others run smoothly only going downgrade. When you hear one knocking all the time, it's a sure sign there is something wrong under the hood.*

Remember this: If you are afraid of criticism, you will die doing nothing. If you want a place in the sun, you will have to expect to receive some blisters and have some sand kicked in your face. Criticism is a compliment when you know what you are doing is right.

Continually Frustrate Tradition With Your Creativity and Imagination

STOP AND DAYDREAM ONCE IN A WHILE. We all need to let our imaginations roam and give them a chance to breathe. It's never too late for you to start thinking more creatively.

Often it is merely a lack of imagination that keeps a person from his potential. Thinking of new ideas is like shaving: If you don't do it every day, you're a bum. Start and maintain a constant flow of new, exciting, and powerful ideas on which you act immediately.

Continually frustrate tradition with your creativity and imagination.

The opportunities of man are limited only by his imagination. But so few have imagination that there are ten thousand fiddlers to one composer.
—Charles Kettering

Your dreams are a preview to your greatness. All men who have achieved great things have been dreamers. It may be that those who do most, dream most. A shallow thinker seldom makes a deep impression. We act, or fail to act, not because of *will*, as is so commonly believed, but because of *vision*. Only a person who sees the invisible can do the impossible.

> *Ideas are like rabbits. You get a couple*
> *and learn how to handle them,*
> *and pretty soon you have a dozen.*
>
> —ANONYMOUS

You'll get more out of every part of your life if you stay incurably curious. "The important thing is to not stop questioning. Never lose a holy curiosity" (Albert Einstein). Dexter Yager says, "Don't let anybody steal your dream."

"We've got to have a dream if we are going to make a dream come true" (Denis Waitley). Nothing happens unless there's a dream first. The more you can dream, the more you can do.

> *Ideas are like the stars: we never reach them,*
> *but, like the mariners of the sea, we chart our*
> *course by them.*
>
> —CARL SCHURZ

God gave us a world unfinished so we might share in the joys and satisfaction of creation: "Creativity has been built into every one of us; it's part of our design. Each of us lives less of the life God intended for us when we choose not to live out the creative powers we possess" (Ted Engstrom).

> *I'm a big fan of dreams. Unfortunately, dreams are*
> *the first casualty in life—people seem to give them*
> *up quicker than anything for a "reality."*
>
> —KEVIN COSTNER

> *Realistic people with practical aims are rarely as*
> *realistic or practical in the long-run of life as*
> *the dreamers who pursue their dreams.*
>
> —HANS SELYE

What you need is an idea. Be brave enough to live creatively. "Since it doesn't cost a dime to dream, you'll never short-change yourself when you stretch your imagination" (Robert Schuller). A single idea—the sudden flash of any thought—may be worth a million dollars. Look at things not as they are but as they can be. Vision adds value to everything.

God Will Use You Right
Where You Are Today

YOU DON'T NEED TO DO ANYTHING ELSE for God to begin to use you now. You don't have to read another book, listen to another cassette tape, memorize another passage, plant another seed gift, or repeat another creed or confession. You don't even need to attend another church service before God can use you.

God uses willing vessels, not brimming vessels. Throughout the Bible, in order to fulfill His plans for the earth, God used all kinds of people from all walks of life:

- Matthew, a government employee who became an apostle
- Gideon, a common laborer who became a valiant leader of men
- Jacob, a deceiver and refugee whose name became Israel and who became the father of the twelve tribes of Israel
- Deborah, a housewife who became a judge
- Moses, a stutterer who became a deliverer
- Jeremiah, a child who fearlessly spoke the Word of the Lord
- Aaron, a servant who became God's spokesman
- Nicodemus, a Pharisee who became a defender of the faith

- David, a shepherd boy who became a king
- Hosea, a marital failure who prophesied to save Israel
- Joseph, a prisoner who became prime minister
- Esther, an orphan who became a queen
- Elijah, a homely man who became a mighty prophet
- Joshua, an assistant who became a conqueror
- James and John, fishermen who became close disciples of Christ and were known as the "sons of thunder"
- Abraham, a nomad who became the father of many nations
- John the Baptist, a vagabond who became the forerunner of Jesus
- Mary, an unknown virgin who gave birth to the Son of God
- Nehemiah, a cupbearer who built the wall of Jerusalem
- Shadrach, Meshach, and Abednego, Hebrew exiles who became great leaders in the Babylonian Empire
- Hezekiah, an idolatrous father's son, who became a king renowned for doing right in the sight of the Lord
- Isaiah, a man of unclean lips who prophesied the birth of God's Messiah
- Paul, a self-righteous persecutor who became the greatest missionary in history and the author of two-thirds of the books of the New Testament.

All God needs is all of you!

Do You Count Your Blessings, or Do You Think Your Blessings Don't Count?

If the only prayer you say in your whole life is "Thank you," that would suffice.

—Meister Eckhart

Do you have an attitude of gratitude? If we would stop to think more, we would stop to thank more. Of all the human feelings, gratitude has the shortest memory.

Cicero said, "A thankful heart is not only the greatest virtue, but the parent of all other virtues." The degree to which you are thankful is a sure index of your spiritual health. Max Lucado wrote, "The devil doesn't have to steal anything from you, all he has to do is make you take it for granted." When you count all of your blessings, you will always show a profit.

Replace regret with gratitude. Be grateful for what you have, not regretful for what you don't have. If you can't be thankful for what you have, be thankful for what you have escaped. Henry

Ward Beecher said, "The unthankful . . . discovers no mercies; but the thankful heart . . . will find in every hour, some heavenly blessings." The more you complain, the less you'll obtain.

> *If we get everything we want, we will soon*
> *want nothing that we get.*
> —VERNON LUCHIES

If you don't enjoy what you have, how could you be happier with more? Francis Schaeffer said, "The beginning of men's rebellion against God was, and is, the lack of a thankful heart." The seeds of discouragement will not grow in a thankful heart. Erich Fromm remarked, "Greed is a bottomless pit which exhausts the person in an endless effort to satisfy the need without ever reaching satisfaction."

Epicurus reflected, "Nothing is enough for the man to whom enough is too little." It's a sure sign of mediocrity to be moderate with our thanks. Don't find yourself so busy asking God for favors that you have no time to thank Him. I relate to what Joel Budd said: "I feel like I'm the one who wrote *Amazing Grace*."

> *Happiness always looks small while you hold it in*
> *your hands, but let it go, and you learn at once*
> *how big and precious it is.*
> —MAXIM GORKY

I believe we should have the attitude of George Hubert, who said, "Thou, O Lord, has given so much to me, give me one more thing—a grateful heart." The Bible says (in Psalms), "Let us come before His presence with thanksgiving" (author's paraphrase). Our thanks to God should always precede our requests of Him. The Bible challenges us in 1 Thessalonians 5:17–18, "Pray without ceasing. In everything give thanks" (NKJV).

"We don't thank God for much he has given us. Our prayers

are too often the beggar's prayer, the prayer that asks for something. We offer too few prayers of thanksgiving and of praise" (Robert Woods). Don't find yourself at the end of your life saying, "What a wonderful life I've had! I only wish I'd realized it and appreciated it sooner."

Thank God for dirty dishes;
they have a tale to tell.
While other folks go hungry,
we're eating pretty well.
With home, and health, and happiness,
we shouldn't want to fuss;
For by this stack of evidence,
God's very good to us.

—ANONYMOUS

WINNING STARTS
WITH BEGINNING

EVERYTHING BIG STARTS WITH SOMETHING SMALL. Nothing great is created suddenly. Nothing can be done except little by little. Never decide to do nothing just because you can only do something.

People who think they are too big to do little things are perhaps too little to be asked to do big things. Small opportunities are often the beginning of great enterprises.

Within a little thing lies a big opportunity. Small things make a big difference; therefore, do all that it takes to be successful in little things.

One of the most frequent prayers I pray is, *Lord, send small opportunities into my life.* I know that if I am faithful in the small things, bigger opportunities will open up to me. When we're faithful in those small opportunities, God says to us,

> *You have been faithful in handling this small amount . . . so now I will give you many more responsibilities. Begin the joyous tasks I have assigned to you.*
> —MATTHEW 25:21 TLB

You will never do great things if you can't do small things in a great way. All difficult things have their beginning in that which is easy, and great things in that which is small.

One of the major differences between people who have momentum and those who don't is that those with momentum are growing by taking advantage of small opportunities. The impossible, many times, is simply the untried. Here's some of the best advice I've been given: "Do something!" The courage to begin is the same courage it takes to succeed. This is the courage that usually separates dreamers from achievers.

> *Winning starts with beginning.*
> —ROBERT SCHULLER

The beginning is the most important part of any endeavor. Worse than a quitter is anyone who is afraid to begin. Ninety percent of success is showing up and starting. You may be disappointed if you fail, but you are doomed if you don't try.

Don't be deceived: Knowledge alone of where you want to go can never be a substitute for putting one foot in front of the other. Discover step-by-step excitement. To win you must begin.

The first step is the hardest. "That's why many fail—because they don't get started—they don't go. They don't overcome inertia. They don't begin" (W. Clement Stone). Don't be discouraged. Little steps add up, and they add up rapidly.

Dare to begin. No endeavor is worse than that which is not attempted. You don't know what you can do until you have tried. People, like trees, must grow or wither. There's no standing still. Do what you can.

> *It is always your next move.*
> —N. HILL

It's As Important to Know What God Can't Do As to Know What He Can Do

GOD CANNOT LIE.

God cannot change.

God cannot recall our sins after we've asked for forgiveness.

God cannot be the author of confusion.

God cannot leave us or forsake us.

God cannot go back on His promises.

God cannot revoke His gifts.

God cannot be pleased without faith.

God cannot be defeated.

God cannot be too big for our problems.

God cannot be too small for our problems.

God cannot prefer one person over another.

God cannot break His covenant.

God cannot revoke His calling.

God cannot be unjust.

God cannot do anything contrary to Scripture.
    God cannot bless a lie.
        God cannot love sin.

God cannot give anything to a double-minded person.
    God cannot be forced into an impossible situation.
    God cannot ignore the praises of His people.

God cannot be our problem.
    God cannot be overcome by the world.
        God cannot be late.

God cannot be neutral.
    God cannot be weak.
        God cannot bless doubt.

God cannot withhold wisdom from those who ask in faith.

Don't Spend Your Life Standing at the Complaint Counter

THE MORE YOU COMPLAIN THE LESS YOU'LL OBTAIN. The person who is always finding fault seldom finds anything else. Therefore, live your life as an exclamation, not an explanation.

Any failure will tell you success is nothing but luck. Children are born optimists, and the world slowly tries to educate them out of their "delusion."

A life of complaining is the ultimate rut. The only difference between a rut and a grave is their measurements. Those who have nothing good to say are always stuck.

> *Little men with little minds and little imagination jog through life in little ruts, smugly resisting all changes that would jar their little worlds.*
> —ANONYMOUS

Some of the most disappointed people in the world are those who get what is coming to them.

Small things always affect small minds. Some people are confident they could move mountains if only someone else would just clear the foothills out of the way.

Misery wants your company. Complainers attract other complainers while repelling positive people. When God gets ready to bless you, He doesn't send complainers into your life. He sends those full of faith, power, and love.

When you feel like complaining, bring God into the situation. You have to shut out His light to be in the darkness: "Thou wilt keep him in perfect peace, whose mind is stayed on thee" (Isaiah 26:3). Is God your hope or your excuse? Don't let heaven become only a complaint counter.

> *Of all sad words of tongue or pen, the saddest are these: "It might have been!"*
> —JOHN GREENLEAF WHITTIER

Don't complain. The wheel that squeaks the loudest often gets replaced. If you complain about other people, you have no time to love them. When you complain, you explain your pain for no gain.

If You Pluck the Blossoms, You Must Do Without the Fruit

GOD IS A GOD OF SEASONS: "To everything there is a season, and a time to every purpose under the heaven" (Ecclesiastes 3:1). Distinctly different things happen during different seasons.

There is a *wintertime* in God. It is a season of preparation, revelation, and direction. It is also the time when the roots grow. God wants to establish the right foundation in you during this season. But there is no harvest now.

There is a *springtime* in God. It is a time of planting, hoeing, and nurturing. In other words, hard work. God wants you to work your plan. Yet there is no harvest in springtime.

There is a *summertime* in God. Summer is a time of great growth. Now is the time when activity, interest, and people begin to surround your God-given idea. For all the activity of summer, there is only a minimal harvest. But then comes autumn.

This is God's *harvesttime*. It is during this season that the harvest is reaped in much greater proportion than the work or activity expended. But most people never make it to the fall. Often they end up quitting along the way because they didn't know what season they were in.

When you understand that God is a God of seasons, it prepares you to do the right thing at the right time. It inspires you to persevere to the autumn. God's Word is true:

Let us not become weary in doing good,
for at the proper time we will reap a
harvest if we don't give up.

—GALATIANS 6:9 NIV

It was spring, but it was summer I wanted—
    The warm days, and the great outdoors.
It was summer, but it was fall I wanted—
    The colorful leaves, and the cool, dry air.
It was fall, but it was winter I wanted—
    The beautiful snow, and the joy of the holiday
    season.
I was a child, but it was adulthood I wanted—
    The freedom, and the respect.
I was 20, but it was 30 I wanted—
    To be mature, and sophisticated.
I was middle-aged, but it was 20 I wanted—
    The youth, and the free spirit.
I was retired, but it was middle-age I wanted—
    The presence of mind, without limitations.
My life was over,
    But I never got what I wanted.

—JASON LEHMAN

"You create a season of success every time you complete an instruction from God" (Mike Murdock). Trust God for a good harvest, but keep on hoeing:

He . . . made every thing beautiful in its time.

—ECCLESIASTES 3:11

God has the right time and season for you.

Do More . . .

DO MORE THAN EXIST—LIVE.
    Do more than hear—listen.
        Do more than agree—cooperate.

Do more than talk—communicate.
    Do more than grow—bloom.
        Do more than spend—invest.

Do more than think—create.
    Do more than work—excel.
        Do more than share—give.

Do more than decide—discern.
    Do more than consider—commit.
        Do more than forgive—forget.

Do more than help—serve.
    Do more than coexist—reconcile.
        Do more than sing—worship.

Do more than think—plan.
    Do more than dream—do.
        Do more than see—perceive.

Do more than read—apply.
Do more than receive—reciprocate.
Do more than choose—focus.

Do more than wish—believe.
Do more than advise—help.
Do more than speak—impart.

Do more than encourage—inspire.
Do more than add—multiply.
Do more than change—improve.

Do more than reach—stretch.
Do more than ponder—pray.
Do more than just live—live for Jesus.

ONLY HUNGRY MINDS
CAN GROW

HAVE YOU EVER NOTICED THERE ARE PEOPLE you know who are literally at the same place today as they were five years ago? They still have the same dreams, the same problems, the same alibis, the same opportunities, and the same way of thinking. They are not moving forward in life.

It's as if they unplug their clocks at a certain point in time and stay at that fixed moment. However, God's will for us is to grow, to continue to learn and improve. The biggest room in our house is always the room for self-improvement.

A famous saying reads: "It's what you learn after you know it all that counts." I must admit that I am somewhat of a fanatic about this. I hate to have idle time—time in which I am not learning anything. Those around me know that I must always have something to read or to write during any idle moment that might arise. In fact, I try to learn from everyone. From one I may learn what not to do, while from another I learn what to do. Learn from the mistakes of others. You can never live long enough to make all the mistakes yourself. You can learn more from a wise man when he is wrong than from a fool when he is right.

Goethe said, "Everybody wants to be: nobody wants to grow." I agree with Van Crouch:

*You will never change your actions
until you change your mind.*

An important way to keep growing is to never stop asking questions. The person who is afraid of asking is ashamed of learning. Life's most important answers can be found in asking the right questions.

We should learn as if we will live forever and live as if we will die tomorrow. It's true what W. Fussellman said: "Today a reader. Tomorrow a leader." Harvey Ullman observed,

*Anyone who stops learning is old, whether this
happens at 20 or 80. Anyone who keeps on
learning not only remains young, but
becomes consistently more valuable
regardless of physical capacity.*

Timothy is instructed: "Study to [show] thyself approved unto God" (2 Timothy 2:15). It's fun to keep learning. Learning brings approval to your life.

Learn from others. Learn to see in the challenges of others the ills you should avoid. Experience is a present possession that keeps us from repeating the past in the future. Life teaches us by giving us new problems before we solve the old ones. Do you believe that education is costly or difficult? Listen to Derek Bok:

If you think education is expensive—try ignorance.

PURSUIT CHANGES
EVERYTHING

ARE YOU STUMBLING TOWARD AN UNCERTAIN FUTURE? Or are you ready to wholeheartedly pursue your dream? There are million-dollar ideas around you every day ... do you see them? You can observe a thousand miracles every day, or you can see nothing. Your big opportunity is right where you are now. As Earl Nightingale said, "You are, at this moment, standing right in the middle of your own 'acres of diamonds.'"

There is a master key that unlocks life's possibilities. Dreams are good, but not good enough. Faith is good, but not good enough. Goals are good, but not good enough. There's only one way to prove your faith, dreams, and goals ... only one way to transform them into a reality. *The pursuit.*

The most important thing you can ever do in life is find a dream worth chasing—and when you catch it, find a bigger one. Pursuit changes everything. It captivates your heart, increases your momentum, unleashes focus, and brings astonishing results.

You will find that happiness is chasing your dreams, not reaching them. A major corporate study of sixty-two business leaders all over the world, from Marriott Corporation to Apple Computers, revealed that not one of the leaders was a classic workaholic as we imagine: grim, driven, enslaved by work but compelled to do it anyway. Instead, they were actually "workaphiles," *lovers of work.* They absolutely loved doing what they did! The right pursuit brought joy and success.

John Foster said, "It is a poor disgraceful thing not to be able to reply, with some degree of certainty, to the simple questions, 'What will you be?' 'What will you do?'" Charles Garfield added,

> *Peak performers are people who are committed to a compelling mission. It is very clear that they care deeply about what they do and their efforts, energies, and enthusiasms are traceable back to that particular mission.*

You're not truly free until you actively pursue and have been made captive by your supreme mission in life.

Unfortunately, the average person's life consists of twenty years of having parents ask where he or she is going, forty years of having a spouse ask the same question, and, at the end, the mourners wondering the same. Martin Luther King Jr. said,

> *If a man hasn't discovered something that he will die for, he isn't fit to live.*

Success always starts with a dream that seems impossible, but when that dream is pursued and worked, it gradually comes true over time. Nothing worthwhile happens overnight. The road to success runs uphill, so don't expect to break any speed records.

Success takes time. Once you get your dream going, you have to maintain its momentum. You can't afford to stop along the way. The hardest thing to do in pursuing your dream is to get it rolling from a standing stop. You want to have to do that only once—the first time.

The world makes room for a person on a pursuit. Like a fire truck with its lights on or a police car with its sirens blaring, people may not know where you're going, but they know you're off to something important. For the tenacious, there is always time and opportunity. Don't be caught out in the backyard looking for four-leaf clovers when opportunity knocks at your front door.

Every morning in Africa, a gazelle wakes up. It knows that it must outrun the fastest lion or it will be eaten. Every morning in Africa, a lion wakes up. It knows that it must outrun the slowest gazelle or it will starve to death. It doesn't matter whether you're a lion or a gazelle; when the sun comes up you'd better be running.

In your heart there is a sleeping lion roaring from the inside out, intently desiring a pursuit worthy of placement by God above. Choose to be on a mission.

> *When you discover your mission, you will feel its demand. It will fill you with enthusiasm and a burning desire to get to work on it.*
>
> —W. CLEMENT STONE

Successful lives are motivated by dynamic pursuit.

A lazy man is judged by what he doesn't pursue. Albert Hubert remarked, "Parties who want milk should not seat themselves on a stool in the middle of the field and hope that the cow will back up to them." The choice of stopping or pursuing is a defining moment in your life.

When a person makes a decision to pursue, the facts don't count. The past doesn't count. The odds don't count. The only thing that matters is the decision to pursue.

I don't know about you, but dandelions pursue me. Everywhere I've lived, at every house I've owned, they've followed me. But I've learned something very important from that pesky little plant. Our daily prayer should be, "Lord, give me the determination and tenacity of a weed."

Dig for diamonds, don't chase butterflies. Life is too short to think small. Pursue and march off the map. Go where you have never gone before.

Nothing brings greater joy to the heart of a leader, parent, or spouse than to see men and women pursuing their purpose in life. Now is the time to climb out of the grandstands and onto the playing field!

Welcome to the pursuit.

Do What Others Say
Can't Be Done

CONSERVATIVE TALK-RADIO-SHOW HOST Rush Limbaugh has a wonderful name for his outlandish tie collection—*No Boundaries*. What a great slogan this makes for living our lives. We should do what takes us out of our comfort zones. Be like David. Find a giant and slay it. Always pick an obstacle big enough that it matters when you overcome it.

Until you give yourself to some great cause, you haven't really begun to fully live. Henry Miller commented,

The man who looks for security, even in the mind,
is like a man who would chop off his limbs in
order to have artificial ones which would
never give him pain or trouble.

Nothing significant is ever accomplished by a fully realistic person.

Tradition offers no hope for the present and makes no preparation for the future. Day by day, year by year, broaden your horizon. Russell Davenport remarked,

Progress in every age results only from the fact that there are some men and women who refuse to believe that what they know to be right cannot be done.

Know the rules and then break some. Take the lid off. Melvin Evans said,

The men who build the future are those who know that greater things are yet to come, and that they themselves will help bring them about. The blazing sun of hope illumines their minds. They never stop to doubt. They haven't time.

Be involved in something bigger than you. God has never yet had any unqualified workers. "We are the wire, God is the current. Our only power is to let the current pass through it" (Carlo Carretto). Be a mind through which Christ thinks; a heart through which Christ loves; a voice through which Christ speaks; and a hand with which Christ helps.

If you really want to defend what you believe, live it. Dorothea Brand stated,

All that is necessary to break the spell of inertia and frustration is this: act as if it were impossible to fail.

Do a right-about-face that turns you from failure to success. One of the greatest pleasures you can discover is doing what people say you cannot do.

KNOW YOUR LIMITS,
THEN IGNORE THEM!

AGAIN, LIFE IS TOO SHORT TO THINK SMALL. Rather, do as Joel Budd encourages us: "March off the map." Most people could do more than they think they can, but they usually do less. You never know what you cannot do until you try. I agree with Oscar Wilde in this:

Moderation is a fatal thing.
Nothing succeeds like excess.

Everything is possible—never use the word "never." Charles Schwaab said, "When a man has put a limit on what he will do, he has put a limit on what he can do."

J. A. Holmes advised,

Never tell a young person that something cannot be done. God may have been waiting for centuries for somebody ignorant enough of the impossible to do that thing.

If *you* devalue your dreams, rest assured the world won't raise the price. You will find that great leaders are rarely realistic by other people's standards.

The answer to your future lies outside the confines that you have right now. If you want to see if you can really swim, don't frustrate yourself with shallow water. Cavett Robert said,

Any man who selects a goal in life which can be fully achieved has already defined his own limitations.

Instead, take Art Sepulveda's advice: "Be a history maker and a world shaker." Go where you have never gone before.

Ronald McNair says, "You only become a winner if you are willing to walk over the edge." Capture Randy Loescher's perspective: "God says, 'Ask me for the mountain.'" The Bible says, "The things which are impossible with men are possible with God" (Luke 18:27).

When you climb the tallest tree, you win the right to the best fruit. Dag Hammarskjöld pondered, "Is life so wretched? Is it rather your hands that are too small, your vision which is muddled? You are the one who must grow up." Gloria Swanson said, "Never say never. Never is a long, undependable thing, and life is too full of rich possibilities to have restrictions placed upon it."

To believe an idea impossible is to make it so. Consider how many fantastic projects have miscarried because of tiny thinking or have been strangled in their birth by a cowardly imagination. I like what Gabriel Victor Mirabeau said when he heard the word "impossible": "Never let me hear that foolish word again."

Pearl Buck admonished, "All things are possible until they are proved impossible—even the impossible may only be so as of now." John Ruskin said,

Dream lofty dreams, and as you dream, so you shall become. Your vision is the promise of what you shall at last unveil.

Somebody is always doing what somebody else said couldn't be done. Dare to think unthinkable thoughts.

Develop an infinite capacity to ignore what others think can't be done. Don't just grow where you are planted. Bloom where you are planted and bear fruit. The famous saying is true: "There is always room at the top."

No one can predict to what heights you can soar. Even you will not know until you spread your wings.

Spirella wrote,

> *There is no thrill in easy sailing*
> *   when skies are clear and blue;*
> *There is no joy in merely doing things*
> *   that any man can do.*
> *But there is some satisfaction*
> *   that is mighty sweet to take,*
> *When you reach a destination*
> *   that you thought you would never make.*

Our Daily Motto: "Lord, Give Me the Determination and Tenacity of a Weed"

ALL GREAT ACHIEVEMENTS REQUIRE time and persistence. Be persevering, because the last key on the ring may be the one that opens the door. Hanging on one second longer than your competition makes you a winner. Become famous for finishing important, difficult tasks.

It's been said that a great oak is only a little nut that held its ground.

> *These troubles and sufferings of ours are, after all, quite small and won't last very long. Yet this short time of distress will result in God's richest blessing upon us forever and ever!*
> —2 Corinthians 4:17 TLB

Too many take hold of opportunity but let go of it too soon.

Don B. Owens Jr. said it so well:

> *Many people fail in life because they believe in the adage: "If you don't succeed, try something else."*

But success eludes those who follow such advice. The dreams that came true did so because people stuck to their ambitions. They refused to be discouraged. They never let disappointment get the upper hand. Challenges only spurred them on to greater efforts.

You will be judged by what you finish, not by what you start. If you don't see results right away, don't worry. God does not pay by the week, but He pays at the end.

"The reward for those who persevere far exceeds the pain that must precede the victory" (Ted Engstrom). It is not success that God rewards but always the faithfulness of doing His will.

If you are ever tempted to stop, just think of Johannes Brahms, who took seven long years to compose his famous lullaby because he kept falling asleep at the piano. Just kidding, but it did take him seven years. I agree with Woodrow Wilson:

I would rather fail in a cause that will ultimately succeed than succeed in a cause that will ultimately fail.

As we have seen, 90 percent of all failures result from people quitting too soon. It takes the hammer of persistence to drive the nail of success. Many people who fail did not realize how close they were to success when they gave up.

When you get into a tight place and everything goes against you, until it seems as though you could not hold on a minute longer, never give up then, for that is just the time and place that the tide will turn.

—Harriet Beecher Stowe

The lowest ebb is the turn of the tide.

You always uncover opportunity by applying persistence to possibilities. When looking at the root meaning of the word *succeed*, you will find that it simply means to persevere and follow through. Any diamond will tell you that it was just a hunk of coal that stuck to its job and made good under pressure.

Once again, the road to success runs uphill, so don't anticipate a sprint. Impatience is costly. Your greatest mistakes will happen because of impatience. Most people fail simply because they're impatient and they cannot join the beginning with the end. You need to keep on patiently doing God's will if you want Him to do through you all that He has promised.

The power to hold on in spite of everything, to endure—this is the winner's quality. To endure is greater than to dare. The difference between the impossible and the possible lies simply in a person's determination.

IF THE SHOE FITS, DON'T WEAR IT

IT DOESN'T HAPPEN OFTEN, but while I was writing *Let Go of Whatever Makes You Stop*, I was awakened in the middle of the night with this thought that I believe was from the Lord: *Don't live within your means.*

Even though it was 4:30 A.M., I was so excited about this idea that I woke my wife and began to tell her about it for several minutes. (She said the idea was great but that she really needed her sleep.)

What do I believe God means when He says, "Don't live within your means"? I believe He wants us to act bigger, believe larger, and associate higher. Your outlook determines your outcome. Consequently, make your plans BIG.

I'm not encouraging you to go wild, to have no boundaries, or to be reckless. Certainly we should spend within our means—but not live there. Talk with people smarter than you. Listen to those more insightful than you. Ask questions of those more successful than you. Lend a hand to those less fortunate than you. Don't stay where you are.

I sincerely maintain that many people who think they are frugal really aren't. Rather, they are full of fear. The label of frugality, balance, or conservativeness is often a mask to cover up a deep-rooted fear in their lives.

Don't make such thorough plans for rainy days that you don't enjoy today's sunshine. Abandon altogether the search for freedom from risk: "Only the insecure strive for security" (Wayne Dyer).

No matter what the level of your ability, you have been given more potential than you can possibly use in your lifetime. Don't let the future be that time when you wish you'd done what you aren't doing now. You need to have a dream to make a dream come true.

When you only live within your means, you can't live by faith. If you aren't living by faith, you can't please God, for "without faith it is impossible to please him" (Hebrews 11:6). Whom God calls, He equips and anoints to do the job.

If the shoe fits, don't wear it. If you do, you're not allowing room for growth. Webster knew all about the ineffectiveness of "living within your means." When you look up the word *means* in his dictionary, among many definitions and explanations, it tells you to see the word *average*. When you decide to live within your means, you are deciding to live an average life.

EXPECT SOMETHING
FROM NOTHING

"FAITH IS PUTTING ALL YOUR EGGS IN GOD'S BASKET, then counting your blessings before they hatch" (Ramona Carol). And, I might add, don't worry about His dropping them. Faith is the force of a full life. I believe that the primary cause of unhappiness in the world today is a lack of faith.

As cited before, Corrie ten Boom says, "Faith is like a radar that sees through the fog the reality of things at a distance that a human eye cannot see." Faith sees the invisible, believes the incredible, and receives the impossible. The Bible challenges us (in 2 Corinthians 5:7) to "walk by faith, not by sight."

So what is faith? John Spaulding said, "Your faith is what you believe, not what you know." Alexis Carrel observes, "It is faith, and not reason, which impels men to action. . . . Intelligence is content to point out the road, but never drives along it." I also agree with Blaise Pascal:

Faith is a sounder guide than reason. Reason can only go so far, but faith has no limits.

Faith releases the miraculous—it is the way to God's divine influence. Tommy Barnett counsels, "Faith is simply when you bring

God into the picture." And, where do we meet God?

> *God meets us at the level we expect,*
> *not the level we hope.*
>
> —GORDON ROBINSON

At times faith is believing what you see isn't so. That's why the Bible says, "Faith is the substance of things hoped for, the evidence of things not seen" (Hebrews 11:1).

Put faith to work when doubting would be easier. Faith is the anchor of the soul, the stimulus to action and the incentive to achievement. Faith will never abandon you; only you can abandon it. Nothing but faith can accurately guide your life. Faith gives us the courage to face the present with confidence and the future with expectancy. It is usually not so much the greatness of our troubles as the smallness of our faith that causes us to stop or complain.

Faith keeps the man who keeps the faith. No one can live in doubt when he has prayed in faith. Faith either moves mountains or it will tunnel through them. Augustine said, "Faith is to believe what we do not see; and the reward of this faith is to see what we believe."

> *All the strength and force of man comes from his*
> *faith in things unseen. He who believes is strong;*
> *he who doubts is weak. Strong convictions*
> *precede great actions.*
>
> —J. F. CLARKE

Faith is necessary to succeed. George Spaulding warned, "Life without faith in something is too narrow a space in which to live." You'll feel cramped your whole life when you don't live by faith.

As your faith grows, you will find that you no longer need to have a sense of control. Things will flow as God wills, and you will be able to flow with them to your great happiness and benefit. Colin Hightower encouraged, "Faith is building on what you know is here, so you can reach what you know is there." Listen to Franklin Roosevelt:

> *The only limit to our realization of tomorrow will be our doubt of today.*

Let us move forward with strong and active faith.

Broken Promises
Cause the World's
Greatest Accidents

YOU CAN'T MAKE WRONG WORK. Thomas Jefferson stated, "Honesty is the first chapter of the book of wisdom." Never chase a lie: If you leave it alone, it will run itself to death. Everything you add to the truth, you inevitably subtract from it. It's discouraging to think how people nowadays are more shocked by honesty than by deceit.

> *Those that think it is permissible to tell*
> *"white lies" soon grow color-blind.*
> —Awson O'Malley

We punish ourselves with every lie, and we reward ourselves with every right action. A lie will add to your troubles, subtract from your energy, multiply your difficulties, and divide your effectiveness.

> *Truth is always strong, no matter how weak it*
> *looks, and falsehood is always weak no matter*
> *how strong it looks.*
> —Marcus Antonius

Never view anything positively that makes you break your word. Make your word your bond.

In the war between falsehood and truth, falsehood may win the first battle, but truth wins the war. "If we live truly, we shall truly live," said Ralph Waldo Emerson. Liars are never free. Horace Greeley observed,

> *The darkest hour of any man's life is when he sits down to plan how to get money without earning it.*

The book of Proverbs says it best: "Dishonest gain will never last, so why take the risk?" Honesty always lasts longest. A lie never lives to be old.

"It makes all the difference in the world whether we put truth in the first place or in the second place" (John Morley). As scarce as the truth is, the supply has always been in excess of the demand. Wrong is wrong no matter who does it or says it. Truth does not cease to exist because it is ignored, and it doesn't change depending on whether it is believed by a majority. The truth is always the strongest argument.

Truth exists; only lies are created. Truth shines in darkness:

> *There is never an instant's truth between virtue and vice. Goodness is the only investment that never fails.*
>
> —HENRY DAVID THOREAU

Truth needs no crutches. If it limps, it's a lie. "You'll find that life is an uphill battle for the person who's not on the level" (Joan Welsh).

"If you continue to do what's right, what's wrong and who's wrong will eventually leave your life" (David Blunt). One businessman had a personalized letterhead that read, "Right is right even if everyone is against it, and wrong is wrong even if everyone is for it."

Consider the words of John Wesley:

Do all the good you can,
  In all the ways you can,
    In all the places you can,
At all times you can,
  To all the people you can,
    As long as ever you can.

Status Quo (Latin for "The Mess We're In")

CHANGE. I HOPE THIS WORD doesn't scare you but rather inspires you. Listen to Herbert Spencer's definition:

A living thing is distinguished from a dead thing by the multiplicity of the changes at any moment taking place in it.

Change is an evidence of life. It is impossible to grow without change. Those who cannot change their minds cannot change anything. The truth is, life is always at some turning point.

What people want is progress—if they can have it without change. Impossible! You must change and recognize that change is your greatest ally. The person who never changes his opinion never corrects his mistakes. The fact is, the road to success is always under construction.

Yesterday's formula for success is often tomorrow's recipe for failure. Consider what Thomas Watson, the founder of the IBM Corporation, once said: "There is a world market for about five computers." Where would IBM be today if Mr. Watson had not been willing to change?

You cannot become what you are destined to be by remaining what you are. John Patterson mused,

Only fools and dead men don't change their minds. Fools won't. Dead men can't.

If you don't respect the need for change, consider this: How many things have you seen that have changed in the past year alone? When you change yourself, opportunities will change. The same kind of thinking that has brought you to where you are will not necessarily get you to where you want to go. Sante Boeve discovered this truth:

There are people whose watch stops at a certain hour and who remain permanently at that age.

Do not fear change, for it is an unchangeable law of progress. The man who uses yesterday's methods in today's world won't be in business tomorrow. A traditionalist is simply a person whose mind is always open to new ideas, provided they are the same old ones.

There are people who not only strive to remain static themselves, but strive to keep everything else so. . . . Their position is almost laughably hopeless.
—ODELL SHEPARD

Mignon McLaughlin said, "It's the most unhappy people who most fear change." When patterns and traditions are broken, new opportunities come together. Defending your faults and errors only proves that you have no intention of quitting them. All progress is due to those who were not satisfied to let well enough alone. They weren't afraid to change. Change is not your enemy—it is your friend.

You Can't Get Ahead When You're Trying to Get Even

Never cut what can be untied.
—Joseph Joubert

When you have been wronged, a poor memory is your best response. Never carry a grudge. While you're straining under its weight, the person with whom you're mad is out producing.

Forgive your enemies—nothing annoys them more. There is no revenge so sweet as forgiveness. The only people you should try to get even with are those who have helped you.

"Forgiveness ought to be like a canceled note—torn in two, and burned up, so that it never can be shown against one" (Henry Ward Beecher). One of the greatest strengths you can display is forgoing revenge and daring to forgive an injury.

He who cannot forgive destroys the bridge
over which he may one day need to pass.
—Larry Bielat

The one guaranteed formula for limiting your potential is

unforgiveness. Hate, bitterness, and revenge are luxuries you cannot afford.

People need loving most when they deserve it least. Forgiveness heals; unforgiveness wounds. When we think about offenses, trouble grows; when we forgive, trouble goes.

Our forgiveness for others brings assurance of God's forgiveness for us. In Matthew 6:14–15 (NIV), Jesus said,

> *If you forgive men when they sin against you, your heavenly Father will also forgive you. But if you do not forgive men their sins, your Father will not forgive your sins.*

The weight of unforgiveness greatly drags a person down. It is a tremendous load to carry in the race we're called to run.

When faced with the need to forgive and forget, never make the excuse, "But you don't know what he/she did to me!" That may be true, but it's more important to know what unforgiveness will do to you.

What really matters is what happens *in* us, not *to* us. Unforgiveness leads to great bitterness, which is a deadly misuse of the creative flow from above. Great amounts of brainpower are used up when you ponder a negative situation and plot how to get even. This kind of thinking is completely unproductive. People who burn bridges will be isolated and alone and will deal with neutrals and enemies the rest of their lives. That's why we should build bridges, not burn them.

Vengeance is a poor traveling companion. Every Christian is called to a ministry of reconciliation (2 Corinthians 5:18). Getting even always causes imbalance and unhappiness.

When you don't forgive, you are ignoring its impact on your destiny:

> *Hate is a prolonged form of suicide.*
> —DOUGLAS V. STEERE

How much more grievous are the consequences of unforgiveness than the causes of it! Norman Cousins summed it up when he said, "Life is an adventure in forgiveness."

It's true that the one who forgives ends the quarrel. Patting a fellow on the back is the best way to get a chip off his shoulder. Forgive your enemies—you can't get back at them any other way!

Forgiveness saves the expense of anger, the high cost of hatred, and the waste of energy. There are two marks of greatness: giving and forgiving.

If you want to be miserable, hate somebody. Unforgiveness does a great deal more damage to the vessel in which it is stored than the object on which it is poured.

Every person should have a special cemetery lot in which to bury the faults of friends and loved ones. To forgive is to set a prisoner free and discover the prisoner was you.

—Unknown

If Envy Had a Shape, It Would Be a Boomerang

ENVY IS THE MOST RIDICULOUS OF IDEAS, because there is no single advantage to be gained from it. An old saying goes, "When you compare what you want with what you have, you will be unhappy. Instead, compare what you deserve with what you have and you'll discover happiness." It's not trying to keep up with the Joneses that causes so much trouble—it's trying to pass them. Washington Allston reflected,

> *The only competition worthy of a wise man is with himself.*

Nothing gets you behind faster than trying to keep up with people who are already there.

If envy were a disease, most people would be sick. Frances Bacon observed, "Envy has no holidays. It has no rest." The envy that compares us to others is foolishness.

> *They are only comparing themselves with each other, and measuring themselves by themselves. What foolishness!*
>
> —2 Corinthians 10:12 NLT

Jesus admonished, "Stop judging others, and you will not be judged" (Matthew 7:1 NLT). Envy is one of the most subtle forms of judging others. Richard Evans said, "May we never let the things we can't have or don't have, spoil our enjoyment of the things we do have and can have." What makes us discontented with our personal condition is the absurd belief that others are so much happier than we are. Thomas Fuller warned, "Comparison, more than reality, makes men happy or wretched."

Helen Keller advised,

> *Instead of comparing our lot with those who are more fortunate than we are, we should compare it with the lot of the great majority of our fellowmen. It then appears that we are among the privileged.*

Envy consumes nothing but its own heart. It is a kind of admiration for those whom you least want to praise.

As an Irish proverb says, "You've got to do your own growing, no matter how tall your grandfather was." You'll find it's hard to be happier than others if you believe others to be happier than they are. Thinking about others all day long results in a distorted view of you and them. Whatever you're doing looks smaller; whatever they're doing looks bigger. They look happier, which makes you sadder. They look perfect; you can't see anything but your own problems. When you're green with envy, you're ripe for trouble.

John Chrysostom reflected, "As a moth gnaws a garment, so doth envy consume a man." Envy provides the mud that failure throws at success. There are many roads to an unsuccessful life, but envy is among the shortest of them all.

Pray Until You Pray

AMAZING THINGS START HAPPENING when we start praying: Direction, peace, love, insight, and forgiveness burst onto the scene. Prayer time is never wasted time. Charles Spurgeon taught, "Sometimes we think we are too busy to pray. That is a great mistake, for praying is a savings of time." A. J. Gordon added,

> *You can do more than pray after you have prayed, but you cannot do more than pray* until *you have prayed.*

"The best prayers have often more groans than words" (John Bunyan). I experienced this when I had many pressing needs all around me. Honestly, I had reached a point where I could hardly pray about my needs because they were so many. The only prayer I could manage was *"Help!"*, and I remember passionately offering it to God over thirty times until I experienced a breakthrough.

Psalms declares, "O LORD, attend unto my cry" (17:1). One of the smartest things I ever prayed was "Help!" When I earnestly said that word, God knew all the other concerns I had without my saying anything else. When you take one step toward God, He will take more steps toward you than you could ever count. He moved to meet my needs, and He will move to meet yours.

Prayer alone proves that you trust God. Oswald Chambers said, "We look upon prayer as a means of getting things for ourselves; the Bible idea of prayer is that we may get to know God himself." Follow Dwight L. Moody's advice:

Spread out your petition before God and then say, "Thy will, not mine, be done." The sweetest lesson I have learned in God's school is to let the Lord choose for me.

Do deep praying before you find yourself in a deep hole.

Prayers can't be answered until they are prayed. Nothing significant happens until you fervently pray; pray until you pray! F. B. Meyer lamented, "The great tragedy of life is not unanswered prayer, but *unoffered* prayer." Byron Edwards encouraged, "True prayer always receives what it asks for—or something better." God's answers are wiser than your answers. As Ann Lewis observed,

There are four ways God answers prayer: no, not yet; no, I love you too much; yes, I thought you'd never ask; yes, and here's more.

"Every time we pray our horizon is altered, our attitude to change is altered, not sometimes but every time. The amazing thing is that we don't pray more" (Oswald Chambers). Unfortunately, nothing is discussed more and practiced less than prayer. Pray with your eyes toward God, not toward your problems. Martin Luther mused, "The less I pray, the harder it gets; the more I pray the better it goes." Frequent kneeling will keep you in good standing with God.

Margaret Gibb said, "We must move from asking God to take care of the things that are breaking our hearts, to praying about the things that are breaking His heart." I've found it is impossible to be prayerful and pessimistic at the same time. Consider the words of E. M. Bounds: "Prayer is our most formidable weapon;

the thing which makes all else we do efficient."

Mark Littleton counsels, "Turn your doubts to questions; turn your questions to prayers; turn your prayers to God." When you pray for victory, God will give you a strategy. Phillips Brooks said, "Prayer is not conquering God's reluctance but taking hold of God's willingness." Prayer is not a gadget we use when nothing else works. Rather, I agree with O. Hallesby:

> *Begin to realize more and more that prayer is the most important thing you do. You can use your time to no better advantage than to pray whenever you have an opportunity to do so, either alone or with others; while at work, while at rest, or while walking down the street. Anywhere!*

HAVE . . .

HAVE . . .

- . . . Peace enough to pass all understanding
- . . . Hope enough to keep your heart looking forward
- . . . Strength enough to battle obstacles and overcome them
- . . . Commitment enough not to give up too soon
- . . . Faith enough to please God
- . . . Fun enough to enjoy every aspect of life
- . . . Patience enough to let faith complete its work in you
- . . . Love enough to give to those who deserve it the least but need it the most
- . . . Focus enough to often say no to good ideas
- . . . Forgiveness enough to never let the sun go down on your wrath
- . . . Honesty enough to never have to remember what you said
- . . . Character enough to do in the light what you would do in the dark
- . . . Gratitude enough to say "thank you" for the small things
- . . . Purpose enough to know *why* and not just *how*

... Perseverance enough to run the entire race that is set out before you

... Wisdom enough to fear God and obey Him

... Responsibility enough to be the most dependable person you know

... Confidence enough to know that you and God make a majority

... Kindness enough to share what you have and who you are with others

... Mercy enough to forgive and forget

... Devotion enough to do the right things on a daily basis

... Courage enough to face and fight any opposition to what you know is right

... Optimism enough to know that God's plans are blessed

... Trust enough to know that God will direct your steps

... Expectancy enough to be on the lookout for miracles every day

... Enthusiasm enough to show that God is in you

... Obedience enough to do what is right without thinking twice

... Direction enough to know when and where to go

... Knowledge enough to have your mind continually renewed

... Credibility enough to cause others to want to work together with you

... Generosity enough to give before being asked

... Compassion enough to be moved by the needs of others

... Loyalty enough to be committed to others

... Dependence enough to know that you need God.

Passion Is the Match
for Your Fuse

GOD HAS PUT INSIDE EVERY PERSON the potential to be passionate. One individual with passion is greater than the passive force of ninety-nine who only have an interest. Too many people have only intrigue with their destiny. In Ecclesiastes 9:10 (NIV) we find,

> *Whatever your hand finds to do,*
> *do it with all your might.*

Everyone loves something. We are shaped and motivated by what we love—it is our passion. If you ignore what you are passionate about, you ignore a part of the potential that God has put inside you. Stop and think about what grabs your attention, stirs your passion, rouses anger, unleashes strong words, and causes definitive action from you.

Nothing significant was ever achieved without enthusiasm. Jesus was a passionate man. He died for us because He loved His Father, and us, passionately.

Most winners are just ex-losers who got passionate. When you add passion/emotion to belief, it will become conviction. And there is a tremendous difference between a belief and a conviction.

Driven by passionate conviction, you can do anything you want with your life except give up on something you care about. My friend Mike Murdock said,

> *What generates passion and zeal in you is a clue to revealing your destiny. What you love is a clue to something you contain.*

Fulfilling God's plan is a passionate idea or it is nothing. "Serve the LORD thy God with all thy heart and with all thy soul" (Deuteronomy 10:12).

> *Without passion man is a mere latent force and a possibility, like the flint which awaits the shock of the iron before it can give forth its spark.*
>
> —HENRI FREDERIC AMEIL

"There are many things that will catch my eye, but there are only a very few that catch my heart.... It is those I consider to pursue" (Tim Redmond). The worst bankruptcy in the world is the man who has lost his enthusiasm. You must first be a believer if you would be an achiever.

Impatience Is One Big "Get-Ahead-Ache"

"TIME SURE CHANGES THINGS," an airline passenger told his companion. "When I was a boy I used to sit in a flat-bottom row-boat and fish in the lake down there below us. Every time a plane flew over, I'd look up and wish I were in it. Now I look down and wish I were fishing."

Being at the right place at the right time makes all the difference. How important is timing? Theodore Roosevelt said,

Nine-tenths of wisdom is being wise in time.

The fact that you're reading this book shows that you want to grow—to get somewhere. Like most of us, you want to get there as fast as you can. But keep in mind that too swift is as untimely as too slow. The situation that seems urgent seldom is. Haste slows every dream and opens the door to failure. "The more haste, the less speed" (John Heywood). What good is running if you're headed in the wrong direction?

It's more important to know where you're going than to see how fast you can get there.

Impatient people always get there too late.
—JEAN DUTOURD

We undo ourselves by impatience.

One of the most frequent causes of failure is impatience in waiting for results. "The haste of a fool is the slowest thing in the world," remarked Thomas Shadwell. Whoever is in a hurry shows that the thing he is doing is too big for him. Impatience is one big "get-ahead-ache."

"There is a time to let things happen and a time to make things happen" (Hugh Prather). Life is lived in seasons, which means we are to do different things at different times. Do the right thing at the right time. A Chinese proverb says,

Never leave your field in spring or
your house in winter.

God never sends a winter without the joy of spring, the growth of summer, or the harvest of fall.

Be a good finisher, and never claim a victory prematurely. The greatest assassin of dreams is haste, the desire to reach things before the right time.

ADOPT THE PACE
OF GOD

GOD IS A PLANNER, A STRATEGIST; He is incredibly organized and has a definite flow and pace. Richard Exley, in his outstanding book *The Rhythm of Life*, shows us that God has a right balance for our lives. There is actually a rhythm He wants us to live by: "Whoever believes will not act hastily" (Isaiah 28:16 NKJV). Laziness is nothing more than resting before you get tired.

Pressure usually accompanies us when we are out of the pace of God. Proverbs 16:9 (TLB) says, "We should make plans—counting on God to direct us." Proverbs 16:3 (NIV) promises,

> *Commit to the Lord whatever you do,*
> *and your plans will succeed.*

Cowards never start, and the lukewarm die along the way. Adopt the pace of God; His secret is patience. All great achievements require time—and He is worth your time. Happiness is the right direction, not a final destination.

Abraham Lincoln, during the darkest hours of the Civil War, in response to the question of whether he was sure God was on the Union's side, honestly answered, "I do not know: I have not thought about that. But I am very anxious to know whether we are on God's side." Again, urgent matters are seldom urgent. If you burn the candle at both ends, you are not as bright as you think.

Never remain where God has not sent you. Walking in the pace of God helps us to be established on the proper foundation. Nothing is permanent unless built on God's will and Word. "Except the LORD build the house, they labor in vain that build it" (Psalm 127:1); "The steps of a good man are ordered by the LORD, and He delights in his way" (Psalm 37:23 NKJV).

> *A Christian, like a candle, must keep cool*
> *and burn at the same time.*
>
> —MERV ROSELL

"The strength of a man consists in finding out the way God is going, and going that way," said Henry Ward Beecher. When God shuts and bolts the door, don't try to get in through the window. There is no time lost in waiting if you are waiting on the Lord. Every great person first learned how to obey, whom to obey, and when to obey.

An anonymous poem says:

> *Or place I choose, or place I shun,*
> *My soul is satisfied with none;*
> *But when Thy will directs my way,*
> *'Tis equal joy to go or stay.*

KEEP YOUR TEMPER—
NOBODY ELSE WANTS IT

DON'T FLY INTO A RAGE UNLESS YOU ARE PREPARED for a rough landing. Anger falls one letter short of danger. People constantly blowing fuses are generally left in the dark. If you lose your head, how can you expect to use it?

A Filipino saying advises: "Postpone today's anger until tomorrow." (Then apply this rule the next day and the next.) When you are upset, take a lesson from modern science: Always count down before blasting off. Seneca quipped, "The best cure for anger is delay." Proverbs counsels,

> *He who is slow to anger is better than the mighty,*
> *and he who rules his spirit than he who takes a city.*
> —16:32 NKJV

Blowing your stack never fails to add to the air pollution. How many great ideas have you had while you were angry? How many "expensive words" have you said when you were upset? You'll never get to the top if you keep blowing yours.

One of the worst fruits of anger is revenge. No passion of the human heart promises so much and pays so little as that of revenge. The longest odds in the world are those against getting even with someone.

Instead of revenge, consider what the Bible orders: " 'Vengeance is Mine, I will repay,' says the Lord. Therefore, 'If your enemy is hungry, feed him; If he is thirsty, give him a drink; For in so doing you will heap coals of fire on his head' " (Romans 12:19–20 NKJV). Francis Bacon added,

> *In taking revenge a man is but even with his enemies; but in passing it over, he is superior.*

Marcus Antonius reflected, "Consider how much more you often suffer from your anger and grief than from those very things for which you are angry and grieved." David Hume said,

> *He is happy whose circumstances suit his temper; but he is more excellent who can suit his temper to any circumstance.*

Anger comes back to you, and it will surely hit you harder than anyone or anything at which you throw it.

Time spent in getting even is better used in trying to get ahead. Revenge is like biting a dog because the dog has bitten you. When trying to get even, you will always do odd and unhelpful things.

> *Vengeance is a dish that should be eaten cold.*
> —OLD ENGLISH PROVERB

THE MAN WITH IMAGINATION
IS NEVER ALONE AND
NEVER FINISHED

CHRISTIANS SHOULD BE VIEWED not as empty bottles to be filled but as candles to be lit. You were created for creativity. Your eyes look for opportunity, your ears listen for direction, your mind requires a challenge, and your heart longs for God's way. Your heart has eyes that the brain knows nothing of.

Make a daily demand on your creativity. Everything starts as somebody's daydream. All people of action are first dreamers. The wonder of imagination is this: It has the power to light its own fire. Ability is a flame; creativity is a blaze. Originality sees things with fresh vision. Unlike an airplane, your imagination can take off day or night in any kind of weather or circumstances. Let it fly!

First Corinthians 2:16 (NIV) says that "we have the mind of Christ." Don't you know we've been given a part of His creativity too?

A genius is someone who shoots at a target no one else sees and hits it.

We are told never to cross a bridge till we come to it, but this world is owned by men who have "crossed bridges" in their imagination far ahead of the crowd.

—SPEAKERS LIBRARY

We should observe the future and act before it occurs.

Many times we act, or fail to act, not because of will, as is commonly believed, but because of imagination. Your dreams are an indicator of your potential greatness, and you'll know it's a God-given idea because it will always come to you with the force of a revelation.

Grandmother saw Billy running around the house slapping himself, and she asked him why. "Well," answered Billy, "I just got so tired of walking that I thought I'd ride my horse for a while." One day Michelangelo saw a block of marble that the owner said was of no value. "It is valuable to me," said Michelangelo. "There is an angel imprisoned in it, and I must set it free."

Other people may be smarter, better educated, or more experienced, but no single person has a corner on dreams, desire, or ambition. The creation of a thousand forests of opportunity can be found in one small acorn of an idea. "No man that does not see visions will ever realize any high hope or undertake any high enterprise," offered Woodrow Wilson.

The Bible says, "Where there is no vision, the people perish" (Proverbs 29:18). Vision is seeing things that are invisible. Not being a person of imagination causes your life to be less than it was intended to be. A dream is one of the most exciting things there is.

EAGLES FLY ALONE;
CROWS FLY IN GROUPS

EVERY GREAT IDEA AND DREAM must be established within you and you alone. There will come times when only you will believe it is going to happen. Can you stand alone? Can you believe when it looks as if no one else does?

John Gardner declared, "The cynic says, 'One man can't do anything.' I say, 'Only one man can do anything.'" Nobody can do it for you. No one *will* do it for you.

Henry Wadsworth Longfellow put it this way:

Not in the clamor of the crowded streets, not in the shouts or plaudits of the throng, but in ourselves are triumph and defeat.

You can't delegate your thinking, dreaming, or believing to others.

Thomas Edison, who claimed he could think better because of his partial deafness, said, "The best thinking has been done in solitude. The worst has been done in turmoil."

Eagles fly alone; crows fly in groups. Know how to get away and separate yourself. Don't belong so completely to others that you do not belong to yourself. The fact is that we're all in this together—by ourselves.

Alexander Graham Bell made this observation:

*Don't keep forever on the public road. Leave the
beaten path occasionally and drive into the woods.
You'll be certain to find something that you've
never seen before. One discovery will lead to
another, and before you know it, you will have
something worth thinking about to occupy your
mind. All really big discoveries are the
results of thought.*

Most big ideas are discovered when you are by yourself. Be sure to
spend some time alone on a regular basis. Retreat to advance.

Don't accept that others know you better than yourself. Great
leaders have always encountered noisy opposition from mediocre
minds. The biggest mistake that you can make is to believe that
others are responsible for your failures and successes. Each of us
will give an account of ourselves, not of anyone else, to God.

There is power in the principle of standing alone. More than
anyone else, *you* must be persuaded. The best helping hand you
will ever find is at the end of your own arm. I believe that God
wants us to learn for ourselves. Mark Twain mused,

*A man who carries a cat by the tail learns some-
thing he can learn no other way.*

The opportunity to succeed, or not, is yours. No one can take that
away unless you let him. Learn to be alone and stand alone, or
nothing worthwhile will catch up with you.

THINK THANKS

BE AGGRESSIVELY THANKFUL. When it comes to living, do you take things for granted or take them with gratitude? Count God's blessings, don't discount them. Thanksgiving is the attitude of a productive life.

No duty is more urgent than that of returning thanks. How long has it been since you've thanked those closest to you? The person who isn't thankful for what he's got isn't likely to be thankful for what he's going to get. Ingratitude never ends.

> *Attitudes sour in the life that is closed to*
> *thankfulness. Soon selfish attitudes take*
> *over, closing life to better things.*
> —C. NEIL STRAIT

People who forget (or never learn) the language of gratitude will never find themselves on speaking terms with happiness.

Thanksgiving, you will find, creates power in your life because it opens the generators of your heart to respond gratefully, to receive joyfully, and to react creatively. William Ward spoke wisely:

> *There are three enemies of personal peace: regret*
> *over yesterday's mistakes, anxiety over tomorrow's*
> *problems and ingratitude for today's blessing.*

Know that you are blessed. If you can't be satisfied with what you've reached, be thankful for what you've escaped. Just last night I was driving to dinner and was completely absorbed in thought about this book. So absorbed that I drove right through a red light at a major intersection. After being greeted by several horns and one man who wanted to let me know with his finger that "I was number one," I pulled into a parking lot to give thanks to God for His protection, even when I am thoughtless. We all have a lot for which to be thankful. For example: No matter what house you live in, wouldn't you rather be there than the best hospital in your city?

Count your blessings at every opportunity. Take some time today to reflect on all you have. The words *think* and *thank* come from the same Latin root. If we take time to *think* more, we will undoubtedly *thank* more.

I like what Dwight L. Moody said: "Be humble or you'll stumble." There's an inescapable relationship between pride and ingratitude. Henry Ward Beecher pointed out,

A proud man is seldom a grateful man, for he never thinks he gets as much as he deserves.

Don't be a person who has a highly developed instinct for being unhappy. Instead, "be glad for all God is planning for you. Be patient in trouble, and prayerful always" (Romans 12:12 TLB). The best rule is: Whatever you are given, gratefully receive it. When you spend your time thanking others for the good things, there won't be any time left to complain about the bad.

Find fifty things to be thankful for today. As you do, creative ideas will spring forth as a result of the mental conversation you are having with yourself. One of the best ways to generate momentum and opportunities is to sit down and write a thank-you note to people who have influenced your life.

The most highly satisfied life can be found in being thankful.

Appreciative words are one of the most powerful forces for good on the earth. Thankful words don't cost much, yet they accomplish more than can be perceived.

Start With What You Have; Don't Wait on What You Don't Have

YOU ALREADY HAVE BEEN GIVEN what you need to begin to create your future. Don't find yourself saying, "If only I had this ... if only this were different ... if only I had more money ... then I could do what I am supposed to do." People constantly overstate the importance of things they don't have.

Never let what you think you can't do keep you from doing what you can do. Prolonged idleness paralyzes initiative, for to the hesitant mind everything is impossible because it seems so.

Do not wait for special circumstances to act; use ordinary situations. We don't need more strength, ability, or opportunity. Use what you have. Everyone must row with the oars they have been given.

> *The lure of the distant and the difficult is deceptive.*
> *The great opportunity is where you are.*
> —John Burroughs

What you can do now is the only influence you have over your future. No one can be happy until he has learned to enjoy what he has and not worry over what he doesn't have.

True greatness consists of being great in little things. Don't grumble because you don't have what you want; be thankful you don't get what you deserve. Walter Dwight remarked,

> *"We must do something" is the unanimous refrain.*
> *"You begin" is the deafening reply.*

Everything great begins with something insignificant. The great people in the Bible were faithful in the small things. In Matthew, Jesus told the parable of the talents. He referred to one servant who had taken his master's money and multiplied it. The master said to that man,

> *"Well done, good and faithful servant; you have been faithful over a few things, I will make you ruler over many things. Enter into the joy of your lord."*
>
> —25:23 NKJV

In Zechariah 4:10 (NKJV), the Lord asks the prophet, "For who has despised the day of small things?" There is power in taking small steps.

Many people are not moving with God today simply because they have not been willing to take the small steps He has placed before them. If you feel led to go into a particular area, you should leap at an opportunity—no matter how small—to move in the direction in which the Lord has directed you. If you are called to be a youth pastor and are sitting at home waiting for an invitation from some large church, you should know that it will likely never come. You need to find the first young person you can, put your arm around him or her, and begin to minister and help them.

Don't be afraid to take small steps. As we have seen, many times the impossible is simply the untried.

I can remember a time in my life when I was frozen with fear at what God had called me to do. It seemed so huge a task that I was unable to bring myself to face it. Then a friend came to me and spoke two words that broke that paralysis in my life: "Do something!" If you are at a point of feeling frozen because of what God wants you to do, "do something!" Don't worry about the goal; just take the steps that get you beyond the starting point. Soon you'll get to a point of no return.

It is right to be content with what you have, but never with what you are. Happiness will never come to those who fail to appreciate what they already have. Don't make the mistake of looking too far ahead and missing the things close by.

You can never get much of anything accomplished unless you go ahead and do it before everything is ideal. No one ever made a success of anything by first waiting until all the conditions were "just right." The Bible says (in Ecclesiastes 11:4 TLB), "If you wait for perfect conditions, you will never get anything done."

It's a waste of time to think about what you don't have. Instead, spend your time immersed in the task before you, knowing that the right performance of this hour's duties will be the best preparation for the years that follow it. Live this German proverb:

Grow where you are planted. Begin to weave, and God will give the thread.

VERSUS

WE MAKE DECISIONS EVERY DAY. We are confronted hourly (or even more often) with options. We must choose one or the other. We cannot have both. We can choose to:

- Be decisive versus indifferent
- Be better versus bitter
- Be enthusiastic versus lukewarm
- Have a "how we can" versus an "if we can" attitude
- Say "get up" versus saying "give up"
- Embrace risk versus security
- Overcome evil versus coping with evil
- Stand out versus blending in
- Measure ourselves by how much we get done versus how much we attempt to do
- Oppose darkness versus coexisting with darkness
- Develop versus destruct
- Obtain versus complain
- Commit versus try
- Create peace versus strife

- Believe in choice versus chance
- Opt for determination versus discouragement
- Grow versus die
- Demand more of ourselves versus excusing ourselves
- Do for others versus doing for ourselves
- Strive for progress versus drift
- Set priorities versus aimlessness
- Accept accountability versus irresponsibility
- Take action versus activity
- Welcome solutions versus problems
- Desire more of God versus more of everything else
- Be in *Who's Who* versus asking "Why me?"

IDEAS GO AWAY,
DIRECTION STAYS

HOW DO YOU KNOW THE DIFFERENCE between ideas that come to your mind on the one hand and direction from God on the other?

There is a persistency to direction. It won't go away; it shows up again and again. The Bible says (in Proverbs 19:21 NIV), "Many are the plans in a man's heart, but it is the LORD's purpose that prevails." In Psalm 32:8 the Lord promises,

> *I will instruct thee and teach thee in the way which thou shalt go: I will guide thee with mine eye.*

Direction is a stream with banks. When we know what God wants us to do, we can have total confidence that what we are attempting is right and that God is on our side. The most far-reaching, challenging direction is the most significant because God is in it.

Direction is a matter of fact; ideas are a matter of opinion. Direction from God is impossible to follow without Him.

Direction is the mother of divine discomfort, something we should have at all times. Divine discomfort is a sensing that God is wanting to direct us, a stirring so that we are never totally satisfied with where we are in God or what we're doing for Him. If you think you've arrived with God, beware. There is always room for growth.

We should be known as a people with a mission, not as a people just fishin'. Evangelist R. W. Schambach puts it this way: "Be called and sent, not up and went." We are a people with a purpose, not a problem.

In Colossians 1:12–13, the apostle Paul wrote,

> *Giving thanks unto the Father, which hath made us meet to be partakers of the inheritance of the saints in light: who hath delivered us from the power of darkness, and hath translated us into the kingdom of his dear Son.*

Be sure to look for areas out of which God is calling you and into which He is calling you. There is a difference between God's will *in* our lives and God's will *for* our lives. God's will *for* our lives includes those things that He intends for every person—salvation, strength, health, peace, joy. But God's will *in* our lives is unique to each individual. One person may be called to live in one place for life while another is called to move six times within ten years.

Never be afraid of the light of God's direction. Maurice Freehill asked,

> *Who is more foolish, a child afraid of the dark or the man afraid of the light?*

Wherever God guides, He provides. And whom God calls, He appoints and anoints to do the work. Lay hold of those persistent directions in your life, and tap into the power of God's will for you.

SOMETHING DOMINATES
EVERYONE'S DAY

WHAT INFLUENCES, DOMINATES, AND CONTROLS YOUR DAY? Is it the daily news, the noisy negative neighbor, the memory of a failure? Or is it God's plan for you, His Word in your heart, a song of praise to Him? Let the plan that God has for your life dominate your day, or something else will.

Mediocrity has its own type of intensity. It wants to control you. Mediocrity starts somewhere and leads to everywhere. It can influence and affect every area of our lives if we let it.

Some temptations come to the industrious,
but all temptations attack the idle.
—CHARLES SPURGEON

A fruitful life is not an accident: It is the result of right choices. Small mounds of dirt add up to a mountain. If you are not alert to pray, the mountain can dominate your day.

- When the news tries to dominate your day, let the good news dominate your day.

- When the past tries to dominate your day, let your vision for the future dominate your day.

- When fear tries to dominate your day, let right actions dominate your day.

- When procrastination tries to dominate your day, let small steps dominate your day.

- When wrong influences try to dominate your day, let the right associations dominate your day.

- When confusion tries to dominate your day, let God's Word dominate your day.

- When loneliness tries to dominate your day, let prayer dominate your day.

- When strife tries to dominate your day, let peace dominate your day.

- When your mind tries to dominate your day, let the Holy Spirit dominate your day.

- When envy tries to dominate your day, let blessing others dominate your day.

- When greed tries to dominate your day, let giving dominate your day.

Let God dominate your day.

EXPECT THE OPPOSITE

ONE OF THE MAJOR REASONS the Bible was written was to teach us to expect the opposite of what we see in the world. "I can't believe my eyes" is a very spiritual statement, since we are to walk by faith and not by sight. The most influential things in our lives are like carrots in the ground, 10 percent visible and 90 percent unseen. Looks are deceiving.

One of God's principles of opposites is found in what John the Baptist said (in John 3:30):

He [Jesus] must increase, but I must decrease.

God says we must give to receive, die to live, and serve to lead. In this world of opposites—what Pat Robertson calls "the upside-down kingdom"—"He who goes to and fro weeping ... shall indeed come again with a shout of joy" (Psalm 126:6 NASB), and "he who loses his life for My [Jesus'] sake will find it" (Matthew 10:39 NKJV).

When fear comes, expect the opposite—faith to rise up inside you.

When symptoms attack your body, expect the opposite—God's healing power to touch you.

When sadness tries to attach itself to you, expect the

opposite—the joy of the Lord to be your strength.

When lack comes, expect the opposite—God's provision to meet your needs.

When confusion comes, expect the opposite—God's peace to comfort you.

When darkness tries to cover you, expect the opposite—God's light to shine on you.

God chooses ordinary men for extraordinary work.

> *God hath chosen the foolish things of the world to confound the wise; and God hath chosen the weak things of the world to confound the things which are mighty . . . that no flesh should glory in His presence.*
>
> —1 CORINTHIANS 1:27, 29

"Did you ever run for shelter in a storm, and find fruit that you didn't expect? Did you ever go to God for shelter, driven by outward storms, and there find unexpected fruit?" (John Owen). How many times have you felt unwise in your life? Don't worry. Look to the Lord—He is ready and willing to move on your behalf. The Sermon on the Mount was preached to lift us out of the valley of discouragement. If you want to go higher, go deeper.

> *Doubt sees the obstacles*
> *Faith sees the way*
> *Doubt sees the darkest night*
> *Faith sees the day*
> *Doubt dreads to take a step*
> *Faith soars on high*
> *Doubt questions "who believes"*
> *Faith answers "I."*
>
> —ANONYMOUS

BE...

BE...

   ...Yourself

   ...Positive

   ...Thankful

   ...Decisive

   ...Merciful

   ...Persistent

   ...Honest

   ...Excellent

   ...Confident

   ...Prayerful

   ...Faithful

   ...Committed

   ...Dedicated

   ...Focused

   ...Forgiving

... Enthusiastic

... Hopeful

... Trustworthy

... Loyal

... Helpful

... Kind

... Happy

... Courageous

... Generous

... Loving

... Dependable

... Wise

... Holy

... Obedient

... Purposeful

... Effective

... Creative

... Responsible

... Devoted

... Patient

... Optimistic

... Compassionate.

LET GO SO YOU CAN LAY HOLD

YOU'RE NOT FREE UNTIL you've been made captive by God's supreme plan for your life. Only those who are bound to Christ are truly at liberty. In His will is our peace.

There is something significant that happens when we become wholly yielded to Him.

The eyes of the Lord search back and forth across the whole earth, looking for people whose hearts are perfect toward him, so that he can show his great power in helping them.
—2 CORINTHIANS 16:9 TLB

"If a man stands with his right foot on a hot stove and his left foot in a freezer, some statisticians would assert that, on the average, he is comfortable" (*Oral Hygiene*). Nothing could be further from the truth. God doesn't want us to live our lives with one foot in His will and one foot in the world. He wants all of us.

Dwight L. Moody said, "It does not take long to tell where a man's treasure is. In fifteen minutes of conversation with most men, you can tell whether their treasures are on earth or in heaven." As a young man, Billy Graham prayed, "God, let me do something—anything—for you." Look at the result of that simple but heartfelt prayer.

Those who can see God's hand in everything can leave everything in God's hands. You must let go so you can lay hold. When you have nothing left but God, for the first time you become aware that He is enough. When you do not keep anything from the Lord, you show your love for Him. "The most important thought I ever had was that of my individual responsibility to God" (Daniel Webster).

The world has rarely seen what the Lord can do with, for, and through a man who is completely yielded to Him. Corrie ten Boom advised:

Don't bother to give God instructions.
Just report for duty.

What and how you worship determines what you become. Anything that changes your values will change your behavior, for better or for worse.

God created the world out of nothing,
and as long as we are nothing, He can
make something out of us.
>   —MARTIN LUTHER

EVERYONE NEEDS
A FAITH-LIFT

FAITH CAN REWRITE YOUR FUTURE: "The only thing that stands between a man and what he wants from life is often merely the will to try it and the faith to believe that it is possible" (Richard De Vos). Faith is like a flashlight—no matter how dark things seem to get, it will help you find your way.

> *Every tomorrow has two handles; we can take hold by the handle of anxiety or by the handle of faith.*
> —SOUTHERN BAPTIST BROTHERHOOD JOURNAL

Regret looks back; worry looks around; faith looks up. Great leaders are almost always people of great faith. God has something for the man who keeps his faith in Him. Your life will shrink or expand in proportion to your faith.

Think like a man of action and act like a man of faith. Prayer is asking for rain; faith is carrying the umbrella. You must first be a believer if you want to be an achiever.

> *Faith, in its very nature, demands action. Faith is action—never a passive attitude.*
> —PAUL LITTLE

Faith is not a pill you take but a muscle you use. Faith is when your hands and feet keep on working when your head and others say it can't be done. Faith is necessary to victory.

By faith you can be decisive in the absence of certainty or in the presence of indecision. It is not daydreaming; it is decision-making. "Real faith is not the stuff dreams are made of; rather it is tough, practical, and altogether realistic. Faith sees the invisible but it does not see the nonexistent" (A. W. Tozer). The world says, "Seeing is believing." Faith says, "Believing is seeing."

Faith is like a toothbrush. Everyone should have one and use it daily, but you shouldn't try to use someone else's.

> *All I have seen teaches me to trust the Creator*
> *for all I have not seen.*
> —RALPH WALDO EMERSON

Doubt is the great modern plague. Even so, faith can cure it. Real faith will refuse to see anything that is contrary to the Bible. It won't look at the circumstances or conditions but the promise.

One Thought Driven Home Is Better Than Three Left on Base

ASK YOURSELF THIS QUESTION: "What am I really aiming at?" Delegate, simplify, or eliminate low priorities as soon as possible. Do *more* by doing *less*. James Liter advised, "One thought driven home is better than three left on base."

There are too many people in too many cars, in too much of a hurry, going too many directions, to get nowhere for nothing.

> *There is so little time for the discovery of all that we want to know about things that really interest us. We cannot afford to waste it on things that are only of casual concern for us, or in which we are interested only because other people have told us that we ought to be.*
>
> —ALEC WAUGH

Without focus, there is no peace. Follow this powerful advice from Paul, who wrote, "This *one* thing I do . . . I press toward the mark" (Philippians 3:13–14). What you set your heart on will determine how you will spend your life. Carl Sandberg said, "There are people who want to be everywhere at once and they get nowhere."

How can you get what you want? William Locke answered,

I can tell you how to get what you want; you've just got to keep a thing in view and go for it, and never let your eyes wander to the right or left or up or down. And looking back is fatal.

George Bernard Shaw wrote,

Give a man health and a course to steer, and he will never stop to trouble about whether he is happy or not.

We know that Walt Disney was successful. Perhaps the key to his success is found in this confession: "I love Mickey Mouse more than any women I've ever known." Now, that's focus!

Vic Braden said, "Losers have tons of variety. Champions take pride in just learning to hit the same old boring winners." Consider what George Robson uttered after winning the Indianapolis 500: "All I had to do was keep turning left."

If you chase two rabbits, both will escape. I believe you find happiness when you are going somewhere wholeheartedly, in one direction, without regret or reservation. Do what you are doing while you are doing it. The more complicated you are, the more ineffective you will become.

Mark Twain said,

Behold, the fool saith, "Put not all thine eggs in one basket"—which is but a manner of saying, "Scatter your money and your attention." But the wise man saith, "Put all your eggs in one basket and—watch that basket."

The quickest way to do many things is to do only one thing at a time. The only ones who will be remembered are those who have done one thing exceedingly well. Don't be like the man who said, "I'm focused, it's just on something else."

SAY NO TO
MANY GOOD IDEAS

ONE OF THE DEVIL'S TRICKS is getting us to say *yes* to too many good things. As a result, we end up being spread so thin that we are mediocre in everything and excellent in nothing. There is one guaranteed formula for failure, and that is to try to please everyone.

There comes a time in every person's life when he or she must learn to say *no* to good ideas. Something that is good and something that is right are not always the same thing. A good idea is not necessarily a God idea. Our responsibility as Christians is always to do the right thing.

In fact, the more an individual grows, the more opportunities he or she will have to say no. One key to results is being focused. Perhaps no other key to growth and success is as overlooked as this is. The temptation is always to do a little bit of everything.

Remember, saying *no* to a good idea does not always mean saying *never*. *No* may mean *not right now*.

There is power in the word no. No is an anointed word. No can break the yoke of over-commitment and weakness. "No" can be used to turn a situation from bad to good, from wrong to right. Saying no can free you from burdens that you don't need to carry right now. It can also free you to devote the correct amount of attention and effort to God's priorities in your life.

Look at the title of this nugget. Past experiences and present situations probably come to mind. You may recall many situations in which "no" or "not right now" would have been the better answer. Learn from these times and keep yourself from a multitude of mistakes and distractions.

Yes and *no* are the two most important words that you will ever say. These are the two words that determine your destiny in life. How and when you say them affects your entire future.

Saying no to lesser things can mean saying yes to priorities in your life.

Would the Boy You Once Were Be Proud of the Man You Are?

LIVING A DOUBLE LIFE will get you nowhere twice as fast. "Thoughts lead on to purposes; purposes go forth in action; actions form habits; habits decide character; and character fixes our destiny," said Tyron Edwards. Proverbs asserts, "A good name is rather to be chosen than great riches." Character is something you either have or are. Don't try to make something *for* yourself; instead, try to make something *of* yourself.

Character is the real foundation of all worthwhile success. A good question to ask yourself is, "What kind of world would this world be if everyone were just like me?" You are simply an open book telling the world about its author. John Morely remarked,

No man can climb out beyond the limitations of his own character.

Never be ashamed of doing right. Marcus Aurelius exhorted, "Never esteem as of advantage to thee that which shall make thee break thy word or lose thy self-respect." W. J. Dawson counseled, "You need not choose evil; but only to fail to choose good, and you drift fast enough towards evil."

There is no such thing as a *necessary evil*. Phillip Brooks said,

> *A man who lives right and is right has more power in his silence than another has by his words.*

Would your reputation recognize your character if they met in the dark? Desire what David requested: "Create in me a clean heart, O God, and renew a right spirit within me" (Psalm 51:10). To change your character, you must begin at the control center—the heart. A bankruptcy of character is inevitable when you are no longer able to keep the interest paid on your moral obligations.

Henry Ward Beecher said, "No man can tell whether he is rich or poor by turning to his ledger. It is the heart that makes a man rich. He is rich according to what he is, not according to what he has." Live so that your friends can defend you but never have to do so.

Consider what Woodrow Wilson said:

> *If you think about what you ought to do for people, your character will take care of itself.*

Excellence in character is shown by doing unwitnessed what we would be doing with the whole world watching.

You're called to grow like a tree, not like a mushroom. It's hard to climb high when your character is low. The world's best sermon is preached by the traffic sign *Keep Right*.

BETTER IS BETTER

THE TIME IS ALWAYS RIGHT to do the right thing.

Be driven by excellence. To be driven by excellence so at the end of each day, each month, each year, and indeed at the end of life itself, we must ask one important question: Have we demanded enough of ourselves, and by our example, inspired those around us to put forth their best effort and achieve their greatest potential?
—RICHARD HUSEMAN

More harm has been done by weak people than by wicked people. Most of the problems of this world have been caused by the weakness of good rather than by the strength of evil.

The true measure of a person is in his height of ideals, the breadth of his sympathy, the depth of his convictions, and the length of his patience. Consider what the book of James says: "Therefore, to one who knows the right thing to do, and does not do it, to him it is sin."

Of all the paths a man could strike onto, there is, at any given moment, a best path ... a thing which,

here and now, if it were of all things wisest for
him to do . . . to find this path and walk in it.
　　　　　　　　　　　　　—THOMAS CARLYLE

The right train of thought will take you to a better station in life.
Eddie Rickenbacker encouraged us to "think positively and mas-
terfully, with confidence and faith, and life becomes more secure,
more fraught with action, richer in achievement and experience."

If you want greatness, forget greatness and earnestly pursue
God's will. Then you can find both. John Wooden admonished,
"Success is peace of mind, which is a direct result of knowing you
did your best to become the best that you are capable of being."
Harold Taylor said, "The roots of true achievement lie in the will
to become the best that you can become." Elevate your personal
standards of quality. To whatever you thought was good enough
for now add 10 percent. Stand for what's right, then you win, even
if you "lose."

The biggest mistake you can make in life is not to be true to
the best you know. George Bernard Shaw remarked, "Keep yourself
clean and bright; you are the window through which you must see
the world." Follow Ralph Sockman's advice:

Give the best that you have to the highest
you know—and do it now.

MIRACLES BEGIN
IN THE HEART

WHEN CONFRONTED WITH A NEW OPPORTUNITY or tough
situation, I usually ask myself, "Do I have a pure heart and a right
spirit?" The prayer of Psalm 139:23–24 (NIV) is

*Search me, O God, and know my heart; test me
and know my anxious thoughts. See if there be
any offensive way in me, and lead me
in the way everlasting.*

The weapon of the brave resides in his heart. Horace Rutledge said,

*When you look at the world in a narrow way, how
mean it is! When you look at it selfishly, how selfish
it is! But when you look at it in a broad, generous,
friendly spirit, how wonderful you find it!*

The Bible counsels us to prove all things, holding fast to those
that are good (1 Thessalonians 5:21).

Margaret Mitchell spoke this truth: "There ain't nothing from
the outside that can lick any of us." James Allen added, "You will

become as small as your controlling desire; as great as your dominant aspiration." Remember this: When you don't have strength within, you won't have respect without.

If a person's aim in this world is right, he will miss fire in the next. Too many children are afraid of the dark, while too many adults are afraid of the light. William Hazlitt remarked, "If mankind would wish for what is right, they might have had it long ago." Roger Babson added,

> *If things are not going well with you, begin your effort at correcting the situation by carefully examining the service you are rendering and especially the spirit in which you are rendering it.*

To know what is right and not do it—this is as bad as doing wrong. Invite trouble and it will show up early. Save yourself a lot of problems by not borrowing any. Here's more insight about trouble: You don't have to get rid of old agonies to make room for new ones. Nothing costs more than doing the wrong thing.

The man who borrows trouble is always in debt. The best way to escape evil is to pursue good. The person who persists in courting trouble will soon be married to it. Go straight—every crooked turn delays your arrival at success.

Joel Budd said, "A hungry heart is like a parachute. When you pull on it, it opens up and saves you." Keep your head and heart going in the right direction, and you won't have to worry about your feet.

CHANGE, BUT
DON'T STOP

WHEN YOU'RE THROUGH CHANGING, you're through. Many people fail in life because they're unwilling to make changes. The fact is that correction and change always result in fruit.

All humankind is divided into three classes: Those that are unchangeable, those that are changeable, and those that cause change.

> *Change is always hardest for the man who is in a rut. For he has scaled down his living to that which he can handle comfortably and welcomes no change or challenge that would lift him up.*
>
> —C. NEIL STRAIT

If you find yourself in a hole, stop digging. When things go wrong—don't go with them. Stubbornness and unwillingness to change is the energy of fools.

"He that will not apply new remedies must expect new evils" (Francis Bacon).

I will instruct you (says the Lord) and guide you along the best pathway for your life; I will advise you and watch your progress.

—PSALM 32:8 TLB

God never closes one door without opening another one. We must be willing to change in order to walk through that new door. In prayer, we learn to change. Prayer is one of the most changing experiences we will ever know. You cannot pray and stay the same.

Playing it safe is probably the most unsafe thing in the world. You cannot stand still. You must go forward and be open to those adjustments that God has for you. The most unhappy people are those that fear change.

You can't make an omelet without breaking eggs. Accomplishment automatically results in change. One change makes way for the next, giving us the opportunity to grow. You must change to master change.

You've got to be open to change, because every time you think you're ready to graduate from the school of experience, somebody thinks up a new course. Decide to be willing to experience change. If you can figure where to stand firm and when to bend, you've got it made. Welcome change as a friend. We can become nervous because of incessant change, but we would be frightened if the change were stopped.

Blessed is the man who can adjust to a set of circumstances without surrendering his convictions. Open your arms to change, but don't let go of your values. People often meet with failure because of a lack of persistence in developing new ideas and lack of plans to take the place of those that failed. Your growth depends on your willingness to experience change.

NEVER SURRENDER YOUR DREAM TO NOISY NEGATIVES

NOBODY CAN EVER MAKE YOU FEEL AVERAGE without your permission. Ingratitude and criticism are going to come; they are part of the price you pay for leaping past mediocrity.

Jesus himself, after healing ten lepers, was thanked by only one of them (Luke 17:11–19). Learn to expect ingratitude.

If you move with God, you will be critiqued. The only way to avoid criticism is to do nothing and be nothing. Those who do things inevitably stir up criticism.

The Bible offers this great promise concerning criticism: The truth always outlives a lie. This fact is backed by Proverbs 12:19:

The lip of truth shall be established for ever:
but a lying tongue is but for a moment.

Also, in Hebrews 13:6, we are told that we may boldly say, "The Lord is my helper, and I will not fear what man shall do unto me."

Never judge people by what is said about them by their enemies. Kenneth Tynan has provided the best description of a critic I have ever heard:

*A critic is a man who knows the way
but can't drive the car.*

We are not called to respond to criticism; we are called to respond to God. Often criticism will present the best platform from which to proclaim the truth.

Most of the time, people who are critical are either envious or uninformed. They usually say things that have no impact whatsoever upon truth. There's an anonymous saying that describes this situation perfectly:

*It is useless for the sheep to pass resolutions in
favor of vegetarianism while the wolf
remains of a different opinion.*

If what you say and do is of God, it will not make any difference if every other person on the face of the earth criticizes you. Likewise, if what you are doing is not of God, nothing other people say will make it right.

Pay no attention to negative criticism. "Trust in the LORD, and do good" (Psalm 37:3), knowing that in the end what you do in the Lord will be rewarded.

FEAR AND WORRY ARE LIKE INTEREST PAID IN ADVANCE ON SOMETHING YOU MAY NEVER OWN

FEAR IS A POOR CHISEL for carving out tomorrow. Consequently, if you're viewing your future from a position of fear or worry, your perspective is inaccurate. Instead, look forward in faith, knowing that the plans the Lord has for you are "plans to prosper you and not to harm you, plans to give you hope and a future" (Jeremiah 29:11 NIV). Worry is simply the triumph of fear over faith.

There is a story about a woman crying profusely while standing on a street corner. When a man came up to her and asked why she was weeping, she shook her head and replied, "I was just thinking that maybe someday I would get married. We would later have a beautiful baby girl. Then one day this child and I would go for a walk along this street, and my darling daughter would run into the street, get hit by a car, and die."

It sounds like a fairly unreasonable situation—sobbing because of something that will probably never happen. Yet we act this way when we worry. We blow a situation out of proportion that likely won't come to pass.

An old Swedish proverb says:

Worry gives a small thing a big shadow.

That's why the Bible challenges us to cast down vain imaginations—because vain imaginations want to grow and grow and grow, eventually affecting every area of our lives. Have you ever noticed that they never stay small?

As mentioned before, worry is simply the misuse of the creative imagination that God has placed within each of us. When fear rises in our mind, we should learn to expect the opposite in our life. This is shown in the Bible; God says, "He hasn't given us a spirit of fear but of power, love and a sound mind" (2 Timothy 1:7).

The word *worry* is derived from an Anglo-Saxon term meaning "to strangle" or "to choke off." There is no question that worry and fear do choke off the creative flow from God.

Things are seldom as they seem. "Skim milk masquerades as cream," said W. S. Gilbert. As we dwell on and worry about matters beyond our control a negative effect begins to set in. Too much analysis always leads to paralysis. Worry is a route that leads from somewhere to nowhere. Don't let it direct your life.

Psalm 55:22 counsels,

Cast your burden on the Lord, and He shall sustain you; He shall never permit the righteous to be moved.

—NKJV

Never respond out of fear, and never fear to respond. Action attacks fear; inaction reinforces it.

Don't worry, and don't fear. Instead, take your fear and worry to the Lord, "casting all your care upon him; for He cares for you" (1 Peter 5:7 NKJV).

Go From . . .

GO FROM . . .

- . . . Burnout to being recharged
- . . . Failure to learning
- . . . Regrets of the past to dreams of the future
- . . . Frustrated to focused
- . . . Seeing God nowhere to seeing Him everywhere
- . . . Prejudice to reconciliation
- . . . Ordinary to extraordinary
- . . . Defective to effective
- . . . Despiteful to insightful
- . . . Whining to winning
- . . . Lukewarm to "on fire"
- . . . Security to opportunity
- . . . Fear to faith
- . . . Resisting to receiving
- . . . Thinking of yourself to thinking of others

. . . Complaining to obtaining

. . . Drifting to steering

. . . Being a problem to being an answer

. . . Trying to committing

. . . Being a copy to being an original

. . . Envying others to serving others

. . . Ingratitude to thanksgiving

. . . Faultfinding to forgiveness

. . . Criticism to compliments

. . . Alibis to action

. . . Procrastination to progress

. . . Hesitation to obedience

. . . Blending in to standing out

. . . Fractured to focused

. . . Taking to giving

. . . Wishing to wisdom

. . . The world to the Word

. . . Being full of pride to being full of God.

The Most Natural Thing to Do When You Get Knocked Down Is to Get Back Up

THERE IS NO OVERESTIMATING HOW WE RESPOND to failures and mistakes. How do *you* respond to failure? Failure does not mean that nothing has been accomplished. There is *always* the opportunity to learn something.

We all experience failure and make mistakes. In fact, successful people have more failure in their lives than average people do. Great people throughout history have all failed at some point. Those who do not expect anything are never disappointed; those who never try, never fail. Anyone who is currently achieving anything in life is simultaneously risking failure. It is always better to fail in doing something than to excel at doing nothing. A flawed diamond is more valuable than a perfect brick. People who have no failures also have few victories.

People get knocked down; it is how fast they get up that counts. As we have seen, there is a positive correlation between spiritual maturity and how quickly a person responds to failures and mistakes. Individuals who are spiritually mature have a greater ability to get up and go on than people who are spiritually immature. The less developed the person, the longer he holds on to past failures. God never sees us as failures; He only sees us as learners.

Paul Galvin, at the age of thirty-three, had twice failed in enterprise. Then he attended an auction of his own storage-battery business and, with his last $750, bought back the battery-eliminator portion of it. This part became Motorola. Upon his retirement in the 1960s, he advised, "Do not fear mistakes. You will know failure. Continue to reach out." To expect your life to be perfectly tailored to your specifications is to live a life of continual frustration.

David McNally mused, "The mistake-riddled life is much richer, more interesting, and more stimulating than the life that has never risked or taken a stand on anything." What is the difference between the champion and the average person? Tom Hopkins says,

The single most important difference between champion achievers and average people is their ability to handle rejection and failure.

Listen to S. I. Hayakawa:

Notice the difference between what happens when a man says to himself, "I failed three times," than what happens when he says, "I am a failure."

Failure is a situation, never a person.

You can't travel the road to success without a puncture or two. Mistakes are often the best teachers. Ecclesiastes advises, "In the day of prosperity be joyful, but in the day of adversity consider." Oswald Avery says, "Whenever you fall, pick something up." The man who invented the eraser had the human race pretty well figured out. You will find that people who never make mistakes don't make much else. You can profit from your errors.

Failure is not falling down but staying down. Be like Jonah, who, when swallowed by a large fish, proved that you can't keep a good man under water. Remember that a stumble is not a fall—in fact, a stumble may actually prevent a fall. Herman Melville wrote, "He who has never failed somewhere, that man cannot be great."

Not remembered for his failures but for his successes, inventor Thomas Edison reflected,

People are not remembered by how few times they failed, but by how often they succeed. Every wrong step can be another step forward.

David Burns said, "Assert your right to make a few mistakes. If people can't accept your imperfection, that's their fault." Robert Schuller wrote, "Look at what you have left, never look at what you have lost." If you learn from them, mistakes are invaluable. Cultivate this attitude and you will never be ashamed to try.

We truly fail only when we do not learn from an experience. The decision is up to us. We can choose to turn a failure into either a hitching post or a guidepost.

Here is the key to being free from the stranglehold of past failures and mistakes: Learn the lesson and forget the details. Have you ever noticed that the devil never reminds you of the lesson? He only wants you to remember the details. Gain from the experience, but do not roll the minute details of it over and over in your mind. Build on the lesson, and get on with your life.

Remember that the call is higher than the fall.

One Action Is More Valuable Than a Thousand Good Intentions

As Jesus was saying these things, a woman in the crowd called out, "Blessed is the mother who gave you birth and nursed you." He replied, "Blessed rather are those who hear the word of God and obey it."

—LUKE 11:27–28 NIV

It is more blessed to be a doer of the Word of God than even to have been the mother of Jesus.

Few dreams come true by themselves. The test of a person lies in action. I have never heard of anyone stumbling onto something big while sitting down. Even a fly doesn't get a slap on the back until he starts to work. A famous poem by an unknown author states,

> *Sitting still and wishing*
> *   makes no person great;*
> *The good Lord sends the fishing,*
> *   but you must dig the bait.*

Realize that nothing is learned while you simply talk. Words without actions are the assassins of dreams. The smallest good deed is better than the greatest intention. History is made whenever you take the right step. Action is the proper fruit of knowledge. Getting an idea should be like sitting on a tack; it should make you jump up and do something.

> *Go to the ant, you sluggard!*
> *Consider her ways and be wise,*
> *Which, having no captain,*
> *Overseer or ruler,*
> *Provides her supplies in the summer,*
> *And gathers her food in the harvest.*
> —PROVERBS 6:6–8 NKJV

Nothing preaches better than this ant, yet she says nothing. You earn respect only by action; inaction earns disrespect.

Some people find life an empty dream because they put nothing into it. Every time one man expresses an idea, he finds ten men who thought of it before—but they only *thought*. Mark Twain observed,

> *Thunder is good, thunder is impressive,*
> *but it is lightning that does the work.*

The test of this book is not that the reader goes away saying, "What an inspiring set of ideas" but "I will do something!"

The devil is fine with your confessing faith as long as you don't practice it. When praying, we must simultaneously be willing to take the action that God directs in the answer to our prayer. The answers to your prayers will include action.

There are people you know who go to church, read their Bibles, pray, listen to tapes, read good books, and are still a mess. Why? They aren't doing what they need to do with what they know.

> *But be ye doers of the word, and not hearers only, deceiving your own selves.*
>
> —JAMES 1:22

You see, when you hear and don't do, you allow deception to enter your life. You allow inaccuracies to gain hold. I believe that God will never teach you something without giving you an opportunity to put it into practice. He doesn't want you to just hear, He wants you to do. The fact is that if you don't do it, you don't really believe it.

The Bible tells us that action gives life to faith (James 2:26). "Even a child is known by his doings" (Proverbs 20:11). Many churchgoers sing "Standing on the Promises" when all they are doing is sitting on the premises. Too many people carefully avoid discovering the secret of success because deep down they suspect the secret may be hard work.

THE LESS YOU ASSOCIATE
WITH SOME PEOPLE,
THE MORE YOUR LIFE
WILL IMPROVE

THIS CANNOT BE DISREGARDED: Who you choose to be your closest friends or associates is one of the most important decisions you will make during the course of your life.

You are the same today that you are going to be in five years from now except for two things: the people with whom you associate and the books you read.

—CHARLIE "TREMENDOUS" JONES

You will become like those with whom you closely associate.

"Friends in your life are like pillars on your porch: sometimes they hold you up; sometimes they lean on you; sometimes it's just enough to know they're standing by" (Anonymous). A real friend is a person who when you've made a fool of yourself lets you forget it. Good friendships always multiply our joy and divide our grief.

Your best friends are those who bring out the best in you. You are better, not worse, after you have been around them.

A good friend never gets in your way unless you're on your way down. He walks in when others walk out. A true friend is someone who is there for you when he'd rather be somewhere else.

The right kind of friends are those with whom you can dare to be yourself, people with whom you can dream aloud. Sometimes a single conversation with the right person can be more valuable than many years of study. For me, my best friends are those who understand my past, believe in my future, and accept me today.

The wrong kind of friends, unlike the good kind of friends, bring out the worst in you. You know the kind I'm talking about: They are the persons who absorb sunshine and radiate gloom. There are people who will always come up with reasons why you can't do what you want to . . . ignore them! Proverbs says,

> *Putting confidence in an unreliable man is like chewing with a sore tooth, or trying to run on a broken foot.*
>
> —25:19 TLB

A friend is someone who knows all about you but likes you anyway. "Treat your friends as you do your best pictures, and place them in their best light" (Jennie Churchill). A true friend will see you through when others see that you're through. Friends communicate at a heart level. There are good ships and there are bad ships, but the best ships are friendships.

A day away from the wrong associations is like a day in the country. Never have a companion who casts you in the shade. You should have the kind of friends that if you start to thank each other, it would take all day. Mark Twain wrote,

> *Keep away from people who try to belittle your ambitions. Small people always do that, but the really great make you feel that you, too, can become great.*

All People Are Born Originals; Most Die As Copies

THE CALL IN YOUR LIFE IS NOT TO BE A COPY.

In this day of peer pressure, trends, and fads, we need to realize that each person has been custom-made by God the Creator. Each of us has a unique call. We should be ourselves.

Because I do a lot of work with churches, I come into contact with many different types of people. One time I talked over the phone with a pastor I had never met and who did not know me personally. We agreed that I would visit his church as a consultant, and as we were closing our conversation and were setting a time to meet at the local airport, he asked me, "How will I know you when you get off the plane?"

"Oh, don't worry, Pastor—I'll know you," I responded jokingly. "All pastors look alike."

The point of this story is that you must be the person God has made *you* to be.

You and I can always find someone richer than we are, poorer than we are, or more or less able than we are. But how other people are, what they have, and what happens in their lives have no effect upon our call. In Galatians 6:4 (TLB) we are admonished,

> *Let everyone be sure that he is doing his very best,*
> *for then he will have the personal satisfaction of*
> *work well done, and won't need to compare*
> *himself with someone else.*

God made you a certain way. You are unique, one of a kind. To copy others is to cheat yourself out of the fullness of what God has called you to be and to do. Imitation is limitation.

Stand out; don't blend in. The majority, many times, is a group of highly motivated snails. If a thousand people say something foolish, it is still foolish. Truth is never dependent upon consensus of belief.

Don't be persuaded or dissuaded by group opinion. It does not make any difference what anyone else believes; you must believe. Never take direction for your personal life from a crowd. Never choose to quit just because somebody disagrees with you. In fact, the two worst things you can say to yourself when you get an idea is "That's never been done before!" and "That's been done before!"

First Peter 2:9 says of us Christians,

> *You are a chosen generation, a royal priesthood, a*
> *holy nation, His own special people, that you may*
> *proclaim the praises of Him who called you out of*
> *darkness into His marvelous light.*
>
> —NKJV

Romans 12:2 exhorts us,

> *Do not conform any longer to the pattern of this*
> *world, but be transformed by the renewing of your*
> *mind. Then you will be able to test and approve*
> *what God's will is—his good, pleasing*
> *and perfect will.*
>
> —NIV

Christians live in this world, but we are aliens. We should talk differently, act differently, and perform differently. We should stand out.

There should be something different about you. If you do not stand out in a group, if your life is not unique or different, you should reevaluate yourself.

Choose to accept and become the person God has made you to be. Tap into the originality and creative genius of God in your life. If you're not you, then who are you going to be?

ACHIEVE YOUR
God-Given POTENTIAL

"Every secret to a successful, passionate life is found in the Bible."

Author Peter Hirsch was a millionaire, a success guru, and a devout Jew—but when he met Christ, his definition of success changed instantly. In *Success by Design* he shares both his own compelling testimony and God's blueprint for passionate living—the kind that leads to a *different* kind of success.

- *Stop trying to fit your faith into your work life.*

- *Start discovering how work fits into God's design for your life.*

- *Learn scriptural principles that unlock the root to purposeful living.*

- *Dare to use them and see how radically your life...and work...will change!*

Success by Design by Peter Hirsch

"HARNESS THE POWER GOD HAS INSTILLED IN YOU." —*Zig Ziglar*, Author of *See You At the Top*

SUCCESS
by
DESIGN

TEN BIBLICAL SECRETS TO HELP YOU
ACHIEVE YOUR GOD-GIVEN POTENTIAL

Dr. Peter Hirsch